DETENTION AND DENIAL

The Case for Candor
after Guantánamo

BENJAMIN WITTES

BROOKINGS INSTITUTION PRESS
Washington, D.C.

Library of Congress Cataloging-in-Publication data

Wittes, Benjamin.
  Detention and denial : the case for candor after Guantanamo / Benjamin Wittes.
     p. cm.
  Includes bibliographical references and index.
  Summary: "Discusses the legal, political, and moral ramifications of the current U.S. approach to handling detention of terrorist suspects and reviews in particular the historical and current uses of preventive detention under American law in arguing for a formal, statutory system of rules to govern detention in the context of counterterrorism operations"—Provided by publisher.
  ISBN 978-0-8157-0491-1 (hardcover : alk. paper)
  1. Terrorism—Prevention—Law and legislation—United States. 2. Detention of persons—United States. I. Title.
  KF9430.W578 2010
  343.73'01541—dc22   2010039948

9 8 7 6 5 4 3 2 1

Printed on acid-free paper

Typeset in Sabon

Composition by Cynthia Stock
Silver Spring, Maryland

Printed by R. R. Donnelley
Harrisonburg, Virginia

Contents

Acknowledgments

I hope very much that this brief volume will be the last thing that I ever publish on the subject of detention, though I somehow fear that it will not. I honestly do not know what it says about me that counterterrorism detention has become a subject close to my heart, but over the past few years, the subject has grabbed me and refused to let go. I have addressed it at every level that I can—from dense doctrinal analyses to detailed legislative proposals to books and newspaper op-eds. This book represents an attempt to break through to somewhat higher ground, to break free of the case details in which this debate often rightly lives and to talk about some of the broad themes and principles that underlie the debate. It is in some significant respects a distillation of prior, more technical work, but it also advances a thesis of its own—one that is decidedly nontechnical in nature.

I have intentionally written it in a conversational style aimed at the general interest reader. I have eschewed notes except where necessary to document direct quotations, legal cases, and statutes. I have tried to discuss the subject of detention throughout at a level accessible not just to lawyers and security specialists but to anyone who cares about finding a reasonable approach to a set of vexing problems. It is really an essay about the gap between where we are as a society on this subject and where I believe we need to be.

My more neurotically devoted readers (there are only a few, I know) will notice that it has some thematic overlap with my earlier book, *Law and the Long War: The Future of Justice in the Age of Terror*, and that in a few areas it reflects some development of my thinking as well. The development is a consequence both of certain changes in my own views, which have been influenced by the work of others in the years since I wrote *Law and the Long War,* and of changed circumstances that I did not foresee at the time. The chief change in my views involves the value and power of the criminal justice system. In the period since I wrote *Law and the Long War,* owing chiefly to especially persuasive work by Robert Chesney, I have come to believe that criminal justice represents a more powerful tool in the government's arsenal for certain types of detention cases than I had earlier assumed—particularly in circumstances like the present, when the number of new detainees in the system has remained small for a protracted period of time. The chief circumstantial changes involve the precipitous decline in the number of detainees in U.S. custody around the world, the adjudication by the federal courts of dozens of individual detainee cases, and a change of administration that did not precipitate a dramatic reconsideration of the premises of U.S. detention policy. In my work, as in the detention policy that it treats, there are some elements of change alongside dominant elements of continuity.

My debt to several coauthors and colleagues, which is a constant that always exceeds what one can express in a few brief paragraphs, is especially extreme in the case of this volume, which draws significantly on their work as well as mine. Two of the chapters adapt highly collaborative work that I had published earlier with others, who deserve a great deal of the credit for the analytical insights, research, and even bits of the text contained in the chapters. Specifically, the discussion in chapter 2 draws pervasively on work that I did with Adam Klein, a law student sent my way by his professor, Matthew Waxman. I am indebted to

Klein for a great deal of the research that the chapter reflects and to Waxman for introducing us. Similarly, the analysis in chapter 3 of the Guantánamo habeas litigation distills and updates a voluminous report of which I was not the sole author. It was written also by Chesney and Rabea Benhalim, and the chapter throughout reflects their insights and efforts as well as mine. To a somewhat lesser but still significant extent, chapter 5 draws on work that I did with Colleen Peppard, who did a great deal of the heavy lifting in designing and structuring the model law summarized in that chapter. Even in a sole-authored work like this, the scope of my debt to those who collaborated with me on the book's constituent parts is hard to overstate.

This is now the third book that I have written or edited at the Brookings Institution, which has supported me in so many ways over nearly four years. Darrell West, who runs the Governance Studies program at Brookings, has been a constant source of unstinting support. My colleagues in the department have been excellent critical sounding boards for key ideas. Janet Walker and Eileen Hughes of the Brookings Institution Press shepherded the manuscript quickly and expertly from completion to publication. And once again, I would be nowhere without the staff at Governance Studies—Courtney Dunakin, Jenny Lu, John Seo, Ashley Bennett, Ellen Higgins, and Christine Jacobs—whose work every day enables mine and my colleagues' work and for which we fall every day further in their debt.

This book benefited in a number of different respects from the work of the Hoover Institution Task Force on National Security and Law. The idea of writing a short, big-picture book on a subject of great density came to me from John Raisian and Peter Berkowitz. Many of the ideas distilled in this volume were first presented around a table in Palo Alto to my task force colleagues. In particular, Chesney and I presented the analysis that became chapter 3 at a task force meeting in January 2010. The task force also has provided generous support for my work in this area.

The manuscript itself was immeasurably improved by insightful comments from Jessica Stern, Mark Martins, Matthew Waxman, Kenneth Anderson, Adam Klein, Jonathan Fredman, and Jack Goldsmith. It benefited further from research assistance and fact checking by Brookings interns Shannon Dobson, Ritika Singh, and Audrey Keranen.

Finally, this book is dedicated to all of the men and women of remarkably diverse politics, in the current administration and the last, who have advocated for candor and have tried to lash us to the mast as the sirens of denial seduce us. There are many of these people—some of them career officials, some of them political appointees, some of them active-duty military officers. Some of them I know personally and am proud to call friends. Some I have never met but have admired from afar. Some I have probably never even heard of. But when the history is written of our failure as a society to come to grips with the project of detention, there will have been many Cassandras. I salute their struggle.

DETENTION
AND DENIAL

Introduction

"The greatest trick the Devil ever pulled was convincing the world that he didn't exist," says the low-grade con man to the arrogant customs agent in the 1995 movie *The Usual Suspects*, speaking of the great criminal mastermind Keyser Söze. The supposedly crack customs agent Kujan listens with patronizing incredulity to stories of the untrackable, invincible Söze, convinced that he knows the truth and that over time he can get the con man before him to spill the beans. Only in the movie's final seconds does Agent Kujan realize that the con man himself is the master criminal—or at least someone who is exploiting his legend. And, having convinced Kujan that he doesn't exist, he disappears: "And like that—he's gone!"

U.S. counterterrorism policy has a bit of Agent Kujan's Keyser Söze problem. The more successfully our forces take on the enemy, the less people believe that the Devil really exists—at least as an urgent public policy problem requiring the sort of tough measures that challenge other interests and values. The longer the United States goes without suffering a mass casualty attack on the homeland, the less apt people are to believe that al Qaeda and its affiliates and offshoots really pose a lethal threat, that September 11 was more than a lucky strike, that terrorism poses challenges that we cannot address through conventional law enforcement means alone, or that the problem ranks as high as other pressing

1

challenges of the moment—challenges that, unlike al Qaeda, visibly threaten harm on a daily basis. Oil spills, job losses, the national debt, China's rise, and North Korea's saber rattling are all visible with the naked eye. We do not have the option of disbelief. Yet the more effectively we conduct counterterrorism, the more plausible disbelief becomes and the more uncomfortable we grow with policies like noncriminal detention, aggressive interrogation, and extraordinary rendition. The more we convince ourselves that the Devil doesn't really exist, the less willing we are to use those tools, and we begin reining them in or eschewing them entirely. And we let the Devil walk out of the room.

In the case of detention, the subject of this volume, I mean that rather literally. Of the nearly 800 men that the U.S. military brought to its detention facility at Guantánamo Bay, Cuba, as combatants in the war on terror, fewer than 180 remained in U.S. custody as of the summer of 2010. Under the administrations of George W. Bush and Barack Obama alike, we have willingly let dangerous people walk out of the room. Most of them have proven to be low-level nonentities who go home and demobilize. Some have been innocent, detained in error. Some, however, have turned out to be if not quite master criminals, certainly people whose release proves a far greater evil than their detention ever did. We have released future suicide bombers and terrorist leaders. And there have been disappearing acts too. Nobody knows at this stage whether we will come to see the number of such individuals as a manageable and acceptable cost of reducing the U.S. detention rate or whether we will come to see our willingness to let large numbers of suspects walk out the door as a folly akin to Agent Kujan's.

Ironically, it is not just the Devil who is trying to convince the world—and us—that he doesn't exist. We are playing something of a similar game with some of those very counterterrorism policies, which—as a result of bad experiences, complacency, and the passage of time—have become embarrassing. We have learned that detention infuriates people around the world, creates difficult legal problems, and troubles our collective conscience. Yet finding ourselves unable to abolish it entirely and unwilling to face the many troubling questions associated with reforming it, we have chosen denial and obfuscation instead: we pretend that noncriminal detention doesn't exist or that we're phasing it out. In other words, even as the Devil is conning us into believing that he no longer exists, we have begun trying to con the world—and ourselves—into believing that we are no longer detaining him.

The Western world does not believe in detention. Even when Western nations need detention, they do not believe in it or want to acknowledge it, and so, over the years, they have developed elaborate systems for pretending that they do not engage in it. The main vehicle for the West's pretense has been us, the United States; in more recent years, the Afghan government has played an increasingly important role in helping the West pretend. None of the United States' major coalition partners in Afghanistan engages in protracted detentions. But then again, why would they? The United States does it for them. While U.S. forces have the authority to hold the Taliban or al Qaeda operatives that they capture, coalition forces do not. Under standard coalition procedures, they either turn detainees over to the Afghan criminal justice system within ninety-six hours of capture or they release them. The result is that, in practical terms, U.S. detention operations and Afghan prosecutions function on behalf of the coalition as a whole. Given that the United States is far more secure from terrorism than is Europe, it seems highly likely that U.S. detention operations have done more—probably much more—to protect European security than U.S. security. Yet not only have European countries refused to participate in detention operations, they also have become the principal critics of U.S. detention operations.

This peculiar arrangement—under which the United States conducts detentions on behalf of the West as a whole while our European allies refuse to participate in those operations in any

meaningful way and energetically criticize them besides—mirrors
the larger relationship between the United States and Europe on
security matters. It is part of a broader pattern of European free-
riding on the U.S. security umbrella. European countries enjoy
all of the benefits of a robust detention policy and incur none of
the costs. The United States neutralizes dangerous enemies who
pose a threat to both European forces in the field and European
civilians at home. At the same time, Europe washes its hands of
a policy that would raise political hackles at home—just as it
does in the United States—and European officials neatly insulate themselves from the very difficult policy problems associated with detention. Indeed, they can publicly take the high road
vis-à-vis the United States and pretend to maintain a pure law
enforcement model for conducting counterterrorism operations.
It is an ideal detention arrangement for a public that doesn't
believe in detention.

We should not wax too contemptuous, however, for we are fast
becoming the new Europeans. Beginning under the last administration and more decisively under the current one, the United
States has moved to rejoin the Western consensus that detention should be conducted out of view and preferably by proxies.
Indeed, U.S. detention policy is moving exactly in the direction of
this obfuscatory model. The announcement, with great fanfare,
of the closure of Guantánamo but not of the less visible detention facility at the Bagram air base in Afghanistan is only the
most dramatic example of the embrace of obfuscation, denial,
and hypocrisy. Both the Bush and Obama administrations had
opportunities to enshrine U.S. detention policy in law—a move
that would have legitimized detention by stating clearly the circumstances under which Congress regards it as appropriate and
will publicly stand behind it. Yet both passed up the chance. Significantly, the Obama administration did so to loud cheers from
its political base. Moreover, the United States increasingly relies

on Afghans and other foreign proxies to handle our detentions in a fashion that closely mirrors the way that Europeans have long relied on the United States.

But in keeping our detentions out of sight, the United States has a big problem that Europe does not have: We don't have an America that can both do our dirty work and absorb our simultaneous criticism to ease our own consciences. While we can pawn off some detainees on local proxies, there is no extrinsic power whose detention needs entirely subsume our own and who therefore will serve all of our detention needs so that we don't have to—even while we complain about it in public. Europe can have a no-detention policy because it knows that the United States will pick up the slack. Nobody, however, will pick up enough of our slack to allow us the same luxury.

We can minimize detention. Through a combination of prosecution, release, proxies, and Predator attacks, we can keep the number of detainees small, at least for now. But at the end of the day, the United States cannot avoid detention entirely, not even under the Obama administration. The Obama administration itself has come to understand that. To protect U.S. security and the security of its allies, the United States simply has to maintain some detention capacity in a world that doesn't believe in the project of detention anymore.

Unsurprisingly, developing a detention policy for such a world turns out to be rather hard. Indeed, the goal probably is not achievable. That point is not yet obvious. On the surface, after all, shame, denial, and obfuscation seem to be serving the United States rather well at present. U.S. forces today are detaining people only when absolutely necessary and avoiding detention through both over-aggressiveness (killing) and under-aggressiveness (taking risks by letting people go). They also are conducting detentions by proxy whenever possible. And when proxies cannot do the job and the United States must detain adversaries itself, it keeps them out of sight: through internment in the theater of operations rather than anything closer to home, Bagram rather than Guantánamo.

For now, at least, this peculiar system seems to be working passably—if less than straightforwardly. The number of people in U.S. detention has been shrinking dramatically since U.S. forces began turning huge numbers of Iraqi detainees over to the Iraqi government, and international pressure on the United States over the issue has declined commensurately. All that has happened without great apparent cost. While some former detainees have presented nontrivial security threats, many have demobilized, proving that whatever risk they posed was manageable by means other than detention. New captures, at least of major terrorist figures, are being handled relatively smoothly through the American criminal justice apparatus or by letting other countries hold the keys to their cells. In the short term, it's hard to see the costs to the United States of its emerging policy of minimizing detention while shamefacedly hiding the residue of Bush-era policies that embroiled the country in controversy.

Yet those costs, I argue, are nontrivial even now and at some point will become acute. As a preliminary matter, there are moral costs to allowing detentions to take place at the hands of disorganized and often brutal local proxies rather than taking responsibility for them ourselves—all the more when a Predator strike obviates a capture entirely. For those not moved by such concerns, there is also a huge cost in terms of lost intelligence to operations that presumptively employ lethal force rather than seek to capture those targeted. Predator drones destroy not only the people that they kill but their intelligence-rich surroundings as well. That is a cost that the public does not see but nonetheless does pay.

A more fundamental point is that a policy based on obfuscation will work only as long as the number of new detainees continues to decline and as long as we have some regional lackey on which to offload detainees. If, all of a sudden, the United States once again begins capturing people by the hundreds and thousands, as it did at the outset of combat operations in Afghanistan and Iraq, it will no longer be able to sustain the fiction that it is getting out of the detention business.

In other words, while circumstances today may hide the costs, they will not do so forever. The longer we insist on a policy based on denial, the greater the political and legal dissonance that will arise when we can no longer keep detention in the shadows. Refusing to defend a tool publicly has the effect of accepting its illegitimacy, and that necessarily induces a crisis when one suddenly needs to use that tool robustly. Using the tool quietly along the way to that point, meanwhile, is a recipe for constant political tension, as the weight of the system's hypocrisy piles up on judges, legislators, allies, and the public at large. We should not defer until we need a detention system the hard questions that inevitably come up in establishing one.

There is, of course, an alternative—but it's an alternative that cuts completely against the direction in which U.S. detention policy has been moving. That alternative is candor—to acknowledge that we are in fact holding both the Devil and many others besides, some of whom may be innocent, some of whom are dangerous cannon fodder, and some of whose intentions and capabilities we just can't determine with any confidence.

This is a book about candor in an arena in which the siren song of denial is loud, omnipresent, and almost infinitely seductive. It is a book about the attractions of the Western consensus that detention is disreputable, a matter of shame rather than a legitimate tool of wartime statecraft. And it is a book about the ultimate necessity of resisting that consensus and facing directly the true needs of the United States in this arena.

I do not mean to suggest that the United States should flaunt detention, use it unnecessarily, boast about it, or needlessly antagonize the allies, domestic political forces, and federal judges whom detention discomforts. That was the style of the early Bush administration, and it did incalculable damage to the government's long-term capacity to use detention as a tool. Being candid about detention is not the same thing as triumphalism. It is not taking pride in capturing and holding the enemy. It is not making a series of bombastic assertions that our detention screening never fails, or that everyone we catch is the "worst of the worst," or that our holding someone is evidence enough of his belligerency. Being candid about detention is emphatically not equating noncriminal detention with toughness to distinguish its proponents from the supposedly weak-kneed advocates of a criminal justice approach. Being candid about detention is not machismo.

It is instead acknowledging that detention is one among many important coercive tools in the U.S. toolbox and that it has a legitimate place in a global struggle against terrorist groups in which military power continues to play a front-and-center role. Candor is the refusal to bargain away detention's legitimacy or to conduct it in the shadows in shame. It is the insistence that detention of various sorts requires clearer rules. It is the frank acceptance that the enemy's refusal to fight according to civilized norms of combat will inevitably augment the error rates associated with both detentions and releases, for which we, not the enemy, will bear responsibility. In other words, candor involves a certain mature acknowledgment that adjudicating detentions is a complex human decisionmaking process that will inevitably fail some of the time, and that releasing people from detention is also a complex human decisionmaking process that will inevitably fail some of the time. It is the acknowledgment that we will detain some people whose detentions we will come to regret and that we will free some people whose releases we will come to regret. Sometimes the hapless con man will turn out to be just a hapless con man, and sometimes the hapless con man will turn out to be the Devil, who convinced us he did not exist. A policy based on candor would begin with these uncomfortable truths and would deal with them up front, not by hiding them.

Candor requires a serious societal conversation about detention—the very thing that we have been striving so long to avoid and that we make impossible when we pretend that we do not engage in detention. It requires us to make hard prospective choices about the allocation of risk: Are we more afraid of relatively broad powers of detention, which may result in the erroneous deprivation of people's liberty and serve as a recruitment tool for the enemy, or of relatively restrictive rules, which may free members of the enemy? Are we more afraid of the injustice of erroneous detention or of the violence that may result from erroneous release? Candor requires us to make those judgments in the knowledge that there will be costs, and it requires us not to feign surprise at the costs when it's time to pay. These are judgments that we should not be delegating to our court system—let alone subcontracting to the Afghan and Iraqi governments.

Candor also requires that we stop making indefensible claims regarding the security benefits that detention can bring. We cannot detain our way to security, and moving small numbers of detainees to the United States will not pose security risks to American communities. There is nothing magically valuable about the facility at Guantánamo Bay.

Candor is hard, and the political economy of candor disfavors its sudden emergence. The systemic obstacles to a more honest discussion of detention are enormous. Neither political party's base wants a forthright discussion of the subject, and both spend huge quantities of money polarizing the debate. No interest group represents candor. Nobody litigates on its behalf. Candor does not fit on a bumper sticker. Indeed, it is hard today to envision the mechanism by which the United States might move toward a more honest discussion of detention—at least until a new wave of captures some day necessitates it. Our inability to face the subject now will make our task then all the more difficult.

My purpose in these pages is both to argue for actively taking responsibility for our detention choices and to map out the contours of a more candid, morally serious approach to detention. I recognize that if our paralysis is as complete as I suggest, the book necessarily takes on something of the quality of an academic exercise—the crafting of a policy strategy for a country that prefers not to have a policy. I have written it because I dissent from this consensus; I object to the consensus; and I disrespect the consensus. If only for the sake of recording that dissent and disrespect and because I believe that denial will ultimately disserve us and that we will have no choice but to face the subject squarely, I offer it as an alternative view.

Toward that end, in the first chapter, I begin with an examination of our current detention policy—its content, its message, and its ultimate incoherence—and I attempt to illuminate both the many ways in which we have contrived to hide and deny detention and the perverse consequences of such a policy. Our denial, I argue, has been bipartisan—it began during the last administration, not the current one—and it has led us to an equilibrium that is easy to confuse with a stable long-term resolution of the detention problems that the country first confronted in the aftermath of September 11. But that equilibrium is, I argue, a mirage, a creature of circumstances unlikely to persist forever.

In the second chapter, I look at both the myth and the reality of preventive detention in U.S. history and law. The practice has not been nearly so frowned upon as is commonly imagined but has instead been sanctioned in a range of areas, unsentimentally and without apology. That point is important because a common argument against establishing detention rules in law is that doing so would, for the first time in U.S. history, legitimize preventive detention—a practice that our constitutional traditions supposedly strongly condemn. But that condemnation, I seek to show, is a myth, and the reality is rather more prosaic: American law countenances preventive detention when society regards it as truly necessary and when legislatures design laws carefully in order to avoid authorizing detention that is not truly necessary. Properly understood, the historical and contemporary approach of American law to preventive detention should liberate, as well as constrain, policymakers; specifically, it should free them to consider carefully crafted detention policies that address real security needs and include appropriate due process safeguards against error.

That sort of system design is, of course, precisely what is *not* found in the context of counterterrorism operations today. In the third chapter, having argued for the basic congruence between such an approach to counterterrorism detention and other types of preventive detention, I turn to the current U.S. system for rule-making in counterterrorism detentions: the Guantánamo habeas corpus cases. I argue both that these cases are creating muddled rules and that they address, in any event, only a narrow range of the important detention questions that the United States faces. They are, for both reasons, an inadequate mechanism for confronting the country's long-term detention challenges.

In the fourth chapter, I look at two key scenarios that any approach to detention based on obfuscation and denial will necessarily fail to address: an acute unfolding terrorist plot—like the case of would-be Christmas bomber Umar Farouk Abdulmutallab and the more recent Times Square bombing attempt—and a situation in which U.S. forces once again begin detaining large numbers of low- to mid-level enemy fighters without having a proxy power on which to unload them. Failure to forge a coherent detention policy proactively to deal with such scenarios, I argue, will result in political and legal controversy when they inevitably eventually occur and will leave U.S. forces and law enforcement agencies without legal certainty regarding how they should be handled.

Finally, in the last chapter, I attempt to imagine what a policy based on candor would look like, arguing that it would involve setting clear rules for several distinct types of detainees—rules based not on where we capture and hold them but on the character of the detainees themselves. In particular, I identify four specific legislative tasks that Congress must take on if it is to devise a coherent policy to regulate the U.S. system of detention, a system that the country cannot avoid developing.

I wish, in short, to argue a simple thesis: Our current stalemate over detention serves nobody. It does not serve the military or any other component of the U.S. government that has to operate overseas. The system's random operation makes a mockery of the human rights concerns that gave rise to the very spotty judicialization of detention to date. Our current system is one whose parts interact in ridiculous and ill-considered ways that create absurd and perverse incentives. It is a system that no rational combination of values or strategic considerations would have produced; it could have emerged only as a consequence of a clash of interests that produced a clear victory for nobody. The result is that it reflects no coherent policy choices. My modest argument here is that we continue to ignore those choices at our considerable peril.

1 | Current U.S. Policy

By the end of Barack Obama's first year in office, the new president's promise to close Guantánamo had become an albatross around his neck. In numerical terms, at least, he had made relatively little progress toward emptying the facility. His much-vaunted order to bring detainees to trial had produced only a single indictment in federal court. Military commission proceedings moved forward at the pace of a glacier—and, as they always had, involved only a small percentage of detainees. Diplomatic negotiations regarding the repatriation and resettlement of detainees progressed intermittently. A process that in the exuberance of the transition and the first days of his administration the president had promised to finish within a year would drag out indefinitely.

What's more, the project itself had become controversial, with Republicans discovering an ideological commitment to Guantánamo and rallying behind it. Magnifying the ranks of the opposition was NIMBYism in Congress, where many members felt far less strongly about the underlying issues associated with detention than about the need to make sure that detainees came nowhere near their districts. Moreover, Congress slapped a series of restrictions on the president's latitude in resolving detainee cases. New laws barred him from bringing detainees to the United States except for criminal trial and required a waiting period and extensive congressional notifications before the administration could ship any detainee abroad. The glib slogan "Close Guantánamo" had, for the first time, met its political match: a fierce commitment on the part of a broad political constituency to not merely maintaining detention operations but to doing so at that particular naval base.

That was a big change over a remarkably short period of time. George W. Bush, who created the facility, had long said that he would like to be able to close it, and his administration had worked assiduously to shrink it, ultimately removing more than 500 of the nearly 800 detainees who had ever been held there. During the 2008 general election campaign, closing Guantánamo had been a matter of political consensus between the two presidential candidates. Senator John McCain, like Senator Obama, promised to shutter the facility. Even during the primaries, the press had largely treated Mitt Romney's promise to double Guantánamo's size not as a serious proposal but as mere political pandering to the hard right, and the idea never availed Romney much as a candidate in any event. The slogan "Close Guantánamo" reflected the endpoint of a policy on which a vast swath of the political spectrum agreed, and that swath also agreed, in broad strokes, on the means: freeing detainees for whom arrangements could be made that did not involve continued U.S. custody, trying detainees who could be brought to trial, and winnowing down the population as much as possible without taking undue security risks.

Yet the slogan also carried an unhealthy degree of ambiguity, for neither Obama nor McCain ever said quite what he meant by it. The promise to close Guantánamo, like many political promises, conveyed different meanings to different constituencies—people heard in it what they wanted to hear. To many of those on the political left, for example, closure signaled abandonment of noncriminal detention and, more generally, a return to the law enforcement model of counterterrorism operations. To those concerned with harmony in U.S. transatlantic relations, it signaled a meeting of minds with Europe over a festering sore in our ties with our closest allies. And to many people offended by a detention site chosen specifically to evade the jurisdiction and scrutiny of federal courts—a problem that those same courts had already addressed—it signaled a re-embrace of the rule of law and an abandonment of a kind of offshore-banking model of counterterrorism detention.

The phrase "Close Guantánamo" can mean any of those things. It also can mean none of them. Indeed, the promise to close Guantánamo, which Obama and McCain both embraced, actually concerned only a single detention facility. Neither candidate promised to abandon noncriminal detention more broadly, to free everyone who could not be charged with a crime in a federal court, or to bring other overseas detention facilities under the purview of U.S. judges. Technically, either man could have satisfied his promise by moving every detainee from Guantánamo to prison ships at the mouth of Guantánamo Bay. Only in implementation would the promise acquire real meaning.

We will never know what McCain's effort to give meaning to the phrase might have looked like. But during Obama's first year in office, the new president clarified his meaning with relative precision. (For whatever it's worth, I suspect that McCain's efforts would have looked similar; any effort to close Guantánamo would have been deeply constrained by circumstances.) It is well worth focusing briefly on that meaning to illuminate the allure of making obfuscation and denial the centerpiece of contemporary detention policy. For in making Guantánamo's closure a central national policy objective, Obama embraced denial as a cornerstone of the future U.S. approach to detention. To make that point vivid, let's start by outlining what "Close Guantánamo" turned out *not* to mean to Obama.

First, to the disappointment of those on the political left but to nobody else's surprise, it did not signify the end of noncriminal detention. While the new administration has modestly adjusted the legal theory under which it conducts military detentions and trivially adjusted the definition of the category of people whom it claims to have the power to lock up, it has by no means forsworn the power to hold suspected al Qaeda or Taliban fighters without criminal charge for the duration of the current conflict. Obama, in fact, reserved that option from the beginning. His original executive order on Guantánamo's closure did not explicitly mention continued noncriminal detention as a possibility, but it made a point of not foreclosing it either.

The executive order required a review of each detainee's case, looking at "whether it is possible to transfer or release the individuals consistent with the national security and foreign policy interests of the United States" and if not, "whether the Federal Government should seek to prosecute the detained individuals for any offenses they may have committed"—preferably in U.S. federal courts. But the order also contemplated that there might be people whom the government could neither transfer nor prosecute and that some other arrangement—what it euphemistically called "Other Disposition"—would be needed for such cases. For those, it directed simply that "the Review shall select lawful means, consistent with the national security and foreign policy interests of the United States and the interests of justice, for the disposition of such individuals."[1]

As the months wore on, it became increasingly clear that "other disposition" meant long-term detention without trial. Eventually, the administration admitted as much, acknowledging that forty-eight detainees would be neither released nor tried. That number, however, low-balled the real figure, for it excluded a group of nearly sixty Yemenis whom the administration would like to send home—either in the short term or as conditions in that country improve. Yet the administration is not repatriating Yemenis right now, and evidently conditions there are not improving. The figure also excluded those slated for trial whose trials will, in practice, never take place because of imperfect evidence or legal difficulties.

So at least for the time being, the number of long-term Guantá-namo detainees is unlikely to dip below 110. And in the absence of progress on Yemen, it will sink that low only if the government can find a home for every detainee slated for transfer.

None of this should remotely surprise anyone who has studied this issue without ideological blinders on. Even the number of detainees that the government would be left holding after review was, in a back-of-the-envelope kind of way, entirely predictable. In the summer of 2008, testifying before the Senate Judiciary Committee without access to any classified information, I offered the following rough guess of what the residual detainee popula-tion would be:

> Nobody outside of the executive branch knows exactly how many current detainees are too dangerous to release yet could not face criminal charges in federal court—because they have not committed crimes cognizable under Ameri-can law, because evidence against them was collected in the rough and tumble of warfare and would be excluded under various evidentiary rules, or because the evidence is tainted by coercion. Without access to a great deal of material that remains classified, one can only guess how many such detain-ees there are. But the number is almost certainly not trivial. Even under the somewhat relaxed rules of the Military Commissions Act (MCA), military prosecutors have esti-mated that they might under ideal circumstances be able to bring to trial only as many as 80 detainees. Excluding those current detainees already cleared for transfer from Guanta-namo, that still leaves roughly 100 whom the military deems too dangerous to transfer yet against whom charges are not plausible. Even if we assume the military is being hopelessly conservative in clearing detainees for repatriation, there is almost certainly still a gap. That gap involves dangerous men who want to kill Americans.[2]

The "roughly 100" figure corresponds almost exactly to the residual population that the Obama administration finds itself stuck with after the Guantánamo review. I quote this testimony not to highlight my own perspicacity, for the truth of the matter is that the prediction required none. That any administration, regardless of party, would ultimately balance security and political risk in a fashion that would necessitate some minimal detention authority was obvious even then, though many observers denied it. And while improved conditions in Yemen might at some point narrow the gap, a gap will remain, as the administration now concedes, and the government will need *some* noncriminal detention authority to fill it.

Second, "Close Guantánamo" clearly does not mean the end of detention without judicial due process protections—or the right of counsel—in a legal black hole beyond the supervision of federal courts. Guantánamo is the most public face of U.S. detention policy, but it is far from unique among detention sites in having been insulated from judicial scrutiny. Indeed, the several hundred people detained there without judicial supervision at the outset of the war on terror constituted only a tiny fraction of the tens of thousands of people detained in Iraq and Afghanistan under various authorities within the laws of war. The detention facility at Bagram was and still is much larger, and at different points various sites in Iraq housed vastly larger numbers of detainees. Detention sites abroad still exist, and they are no more subject to judicial supervision or process than they were before the president initiated Guantánamo's closure. Indeed, while the Obama administration has created new internal review mechanisms for detainees at Bagram, it has continued to defend the propriety of resisting their supervision by the courts. In May 2010, the D.C. Circuit Court of Appeals affirmed the administration's claim that no U.S. court had jurisdiction over Bagram detainees.[3] Closing Guantánamo, in other words, does not signify a general embrace of extensive judicial process for wartime detainees.

Third, at least so far, closing Guantánamo also has not signified an effort of the type that I have urged to place detention on a more solid legal footing by enshrining it in statutory law and thereby both constraining and legitimizing its use. For a time, that seemed to be what Obama meant to do. At a major address at the National Archives in May 2009, he declared that

> our goal is to construct a legitimate legal framework for the remaining Guantánamo detainees that cannot be transferred. Our goal is not to avoid a legitimate legal framework. In our constitutional system, prolonged detention should not be the decision of any one man. If and when we determine that the United States must hold individuals to keep them from carrying out an act of war, we will do so within a system that involves judicial and congressional oversight. And so, going forward, *my administration will work with Congress to develop an appropriate legal regime so that our efforts are consistent with our values and our Constitution* [emphasis added].[4]

It was a breakthrough statement about detention for a U.S. president, the first time that either Obama or his predecessor had described the future of detention policy in terms of crafting a legal regime to authorize and regulate detention. Unfortunately, within a few short months, the administration had dropped that particular ball. It made it clear that it did not mean to seek legislation after all; instead, it meant to continue to rely on a vague congressional authorization to use military force against al Qaeda and the Taliban as its legal basis for holding the enemy—an authorization that does not even mention detention, let alone set rules for it. It would instead allow the rules for detention to emerge through habeas corpus challenges at Guantánamo, rather than through any deliberative legislative process. The result, in short, was that closing Guantánamo would imply no change in the legal status of any detainee. Bringing Guantánamo detainees to the United

States—if and when that happened—would neither grant them any more judicial review than they received before nor in any significant respect change the character of the review. It would, in fact, change neither the substantive rules nor the procedures associated with detention—just the location.

So what then is Obama really saying to the nation and to the world when he declares that he will close Guantánamo—or, rather, when he declares its closure to be a matter of national policy to be effectuated in due course, though by no specific date? If he is not renouncing detention as a practice by insisting that all military detentions be supervised by the courts or trying to alter the legal basis for detention, what exactly does "Close Guantánamo" mean? The answer, if we are honest about it, is that to close Guantánamo in the absence of a larger rethinking of U.S. detention policy is a complicated symbolic gesture, one replete with conflicting signals. On the one hand, it increases accountability in the U.S. practice of detention, bringing people home whom we now store off shore. It retires a symbol that damages us abroad and damages our self-image. And it signals to the world that we share the values that gave rise to the anxieties over the facility in the first place.

Yet it does all of that by embracing another symbolic element—one that the United States should not so easily accept. It embraces the notion that detention is a matter of shame, to be conducted, for almost all detainees, as invisibly as possible. The administration intends, at some point, to move the dwindling population of this single detention facility to a detention facility in Illinois in the hope that the Illinois facility will be less of a diplomatic sore point than Guantánamo has been. In other words, it means to close the most visible symbol of U.S. detention policy—accepting at some level that there is something lawless and disreputable about it. In exchange, it asks the world to forget about the much larger number of detainees elsewhere, whom we will not talk about if the world doesn't talk about them.

Closing Guantánamo, in other words, is not a repudiation of detention. It is a repudiation of detention at Guantánamo, a repudiation of detention in the open. Obama may or may not take a bit more risk than the Bush administration did in releasing some detainees. He means to bring more of the remaining detainees to trial than did the prior administration, and, at least initially, he tended to favor federal courts over military commissions as the forum for doing so. But the most significant change has been, in fact, geographic and symbolic. And the symbolism is very peculiar.

I have long argued for a policy focused on rules, not facilities, on the theory that *where* a nation detains its adversaries doesn't matter nearly as much as *how* it does so. As a result, I have no particular commitment to maintaining Guantánamo and have never argued against closing it. While it has certain logistical and legal advantages over alternative facilities in the United States and the costs associated with replacing it will not be trivial, those who have to represent U.S. foreign policy abroad describe Guantánamo with near unanimity as a problem for them in the exercise of their duties, and I do not resist the notion that it has outlived its usefulness.

That said, it is worth pausing to consider the oddity of regarding this particular operation with such shame that shuttering it has become a national imperative. In his National Archives speech, Obama described Guantánamo's continued operation as "set[ting] back the moral authority that is America's strongest currency in the world." Rhetoric like that has been common in his administration, which frequently refers to closing the facility as a national security imperative. Yet Guantánamo, after all, is the military's most open detention facility, the one most exposed to sustained public scrutiny. It is the only facility regularly toured by hundreds of journalists and human rights organizations. It is the only facility whose detainees meet regularly with counsel and whose incarcerations are supervised by federal judges. By most detainee accounts, conditions at the facility were dramatically better than those at the internment facilities where they were previously held. Allegations of abuse at Guantánamo itself, for all the attention that they received, were comparatively rare and exhaustively and publicly reviewed. On the merits alone, one might expect human rights groups to demand Guantánamo's emulation, not its closure. How much better life would have been for the tens of thousands of detainees held by U.S. forces overseas since the beginning of the war on terror had conditions at Guantánamo been a broader norm rather than a sui generis oddity! Why should any human rights activist see its closure, combined with the maintenance of a much larger facility elsewhere that is not subject to comparable scrutiny, as a victory?

The same qualities that should have made Guantánamo increasingly attractive over time also made it visible. And the more that American elites and courts and foreign allies came to disbelieve in—and to be discomforted by—strong counterterrorism measures, the more its visibility bred not pride but shame. That began, of course, long before Obama. Though the Bush administration never committed itself to closing Guantánamo, it made the original judgment that large-scale, high-visibility detention hurt U.S. interests more than it helped—and that it hurt enough to take risks to reduce detention's footprint. Over time, then, the Bush administration began to look for ways to obfuscate the detention that we engage in. Early on, it largely stopped bringing people to Guantánamo, and it made the lion's share of the transfers from the facility, removing more than 530 detainees from the base over the years. The mass repatriation of the facility's Saudis was a project of the Bush, not the Obama, administration. The process of moving detention out of the light and into the shadows was well under way by the time that Obama took office. The decision to close the facility entirely was more the acceleration of an existing trend than a dramatic policy shift.

Indeed, over time, U.S. detention policy, even before the Obama administration, came to look more and more like that of the

European countries that had long used U.S. and Afghan forces as their proxy detention system. For example, now U.S. forces also turn detainees over to the Afghan criminal justice system, and the United States built the government of President Hamid Karzai a detention facility to handle returned detainees. The United States also has turned tens of thousands of Iraqi detainees over to Iraq's criminal justice system. Some of that reflects, particularly in the Iraqi context, the turning over of responsibility to an increasingly capable government that ultimately has to run its own affairs. As such, it is a good thing, to be cheered. But it also reflects U.S. shame at the project of detention. Detainees in Iraqi or Afghan custody cannot file habeas corpus lawsuits, after all; they do not generate domestic political controversy; and they do not draw flak directed at the United States from human rights groups. To put the matter bluntly, they are not our problem. It turns out that we are almost as happy as the Europeans are to make arrangements that give us the benefits of detention without requiring us to engage in it.

The consequences, of course, are more than somewhat perverse. Neither the Afghan nor the Iraqi governments hold detainees in conditions anywhere near the norm for U.S. detention operations. Moreover, the desire to keep detention to a minimum probably creates perverse incentives for rendition and targeted killing, a practice that has escalated dramatically in recent years. Indeed, in his State of the Union address in January 2010, President Obama apparently found Guantánamo too shameful even to mention. But the president did boast that "in the last year, hundreds of Al Qaeda's fighters and affiliates, including many senior leaders, have been captured or killed—far more than in 2008."[5] Very few of those people have been captured; to be precise, it is the killing part that's on the rise and that the president was boasting of boosting in his first year in office.

It is a dubious victory indeed for human rights if U.S. forces are now killing people that they used to capture. But dead people do not file habeas lawsuits either—and strangely, perhaps, they do not attract the same kind of sustained political attention that prisoners do. A Predator drone attack makes the news for a day or two, and the story is often of the triumphant "We got him!" variety. While military targeting, like detention, produces its share of errors and collateral damage, the erroneously targeted do not have time to protest their innocence or to gin up public sympathy, and they do not have legions of American lawyers eager to make them into the next cause du jour. Though it yields a suboptimal outcome from the point of view of both intelligence gathering and human rights, these days a kill is, in legal terms, a far cleaner outcome than a capture.

I do not mean to suggest that U.S. forces have made anything so crude as a decision to take no prisoners—or that as a matter of policy we are now killing people that we used to capture because of the legal and political difficulties associated with detaining them. The Predator's rise in Pakistan had other strategic origins—most important, the need to project force into areas with a minimal U.S. troop presence and where overt, acknowledged U.S. military action was not a viable option. It does a disservice to the many men and women in the U.S. military who strive every day to deploy the minimum lethal force necessary to suggest that they calculate matters quite so ruthlessly. Still, rules create incentives, and the increasing prevalence of kill operations rather than captures is probably not altogether unrelated to the fundamental change in the incentive structure facing our fighters and covert operatives.

David Kris, the assistant attorney general for national security, aptly stated the general tension between capture operations and kill operations in a June 2010 speech. "If you're in the Defense Department in the military, and you're thinking about what to do with a terrorist whom you identified somewhere abroad, on the battlefield or elsewhere, you can basically do a couple of different things," he said. "You can do a straight operation to kill him, assuming this is all legal . . . and within the law of war.

That is relatively low risk compared to the other option; it may have a higher chance of success than a capture operation, which is the main alternative. By and large, it's easier and lower risk to kill him than it is to put people in and try to capture him." The kill operation, he said, "will have a higher chance of success in incapacitating this enemy combatant [or] terrorist, but obviously you won't be doing any interrogation and intelligence collection." By contrast, the capture operation is both higher risk and promises a higher payout: "You'll capture him, and he'll be incapacitated through detention rather than death. But he'll also be available for you to interrogate, and that might give you intelligence collection."[6]

In 2002, the United States had fairly liberal interrogation rules that in some instances at least bordered on torture, if they did not quite cross the line. The premise was that they facilitated intelligence collection; it also was assumed that detention posed no great legal problem. Today, however, the interrogation options are notably narrower and substantial hurdles encumber long-term detention. I suspect that those facts bear some relation, albeit not a dominant one, to our apparently increased willingness to kill enemies rather than risk forces to capture them. They certainly should, in my judgment anyway. It's one thing to risk forces to capture someone if the fruits of interrogation are likely to be valuable and one can secure one's interest in incapacitating that person by means other than killing him. It's quite another thing to risk forces in order to buy nothing more than a long-term habeas battle.

It's worth dwelling at least momentarily on the costs of this shift, invisible though they may be. The first of them is a moral cost, and it is, at one level, obvious. Creating incentives to kill people or to encourage their detention by proxy forces under worse conditions to avoid the burden of managing their detention under the humanitarian and legal standards that American values demand elevates the appearance of humane treatment over the fact of it. Taking that approach involves a kind of moral preening that has less to do with human rights than it does with public relations. Its attraction for the U.S. government, which has to think about its human rights reputation as well as the real consequences of its policies for human rights, is understandable. Its attraction for international human rights organizations, which presumably would prefer real improvements in human rights to optical illusions, is far less clear.

A more subtle aspect of the moral cost is the reversal of a half-century's worth of settled understanding in international law of the relative evils of capturing and of killing the enemy. The laws of war traditionally have made holding people in detention reasonably easy precisely to promote their capture, which was regarded as the lesser use of force in military conflicts. The norms and customs of warfare—civilized warfare at least—are overwhelmingly consistent on that point. Due process in military detention is somewhere between rudimentary and nonexistent precisely to ensure that detention is easy; at the same time, it is a war crime to kill someone who has lawfully surrendered. The law, in other words, while unapologetically preserving the right of combatants to target each other without warning, has also traditionally sought to both ensure the availability of detention as an alternative to violence and, once surrender has taken place, to make its use mandatory.

The past few years have turned those presumptions on their heads. We have made detention difficult—shrouding it in shame and attaching to it due process requirements imported from other areas of law—with the predictable result that we have shifted the cost-benefit balance toward greater operational lethality. That is not a trade-off about which we should feel sanguine. It's an erosion of the venerable principle of proportionality in warfare—that a country should not use more force than is necessary to accomplish its military objectives—undertaken to flatter our consciences and to indulge the pretense that we are getting out of the detention business.

The intelligence costs are almost certainly significant as well—and they too have both obvious and subtle dimensions. The obvious one is that dead people don't make good intelligence sources; a drone strike or other lethal action precludes the option of long-term interrogation. The less obvious one is the destruction of the site itself. Some of the most valuable intelligence that U.S. forces gather is not human intelligence associated with interrogation but material collected at the site of high-value captures. Computer files, paper records, contact lists, and the like can be a gold mine of intelligence. Blowing them up represents a significant sacrifice.

It bears emphasizing that situations that demand a decision between the two options arise frequently—even in the current environment, in which U.S. authorities have access to proxy detention forces carefully cultivated over many years. Using information in public sources, Benjamin Powell, former general counsel to the director of national intelligence, estimates that "there was an average of more than one capture operation a month undertaken by the government" in the years since September 11 in relatively high-value cases—though those "were far more concentrated immediately after 2001 as the U.S. encountered al Qaeda members in Afghanistan as part of combat operations." It is possible, he notes, that "capture operations are continuing when targets of opportunity present themselves and we are generally unaware of them" but "public reporting suggests this is unlikely." The result, Powell concludes, is that we are likely losing "incredibly valuable—and rare—information that only human intelligence can provide at times. How does a terrorist cell work? How is it funded? Who are the leaders? What are their plans? How do they communicate? What did a terrorist have with him when captured? Dead men tell none of these tales—and their communication devices and any papers are likely to be incinerated along with the terrorists in a strike."[7] Our lack of stable, well-understood detention rules militates toward the option that involves both greater use of force and less effective intelligence collection.

That is the equilibrium toward which we have drifted, and it should surprise nobody, for it is an entirely foreseeable consequence of the incentive structure that we have created. Imagine for a moment that you had described the direction of our legal policy choices to a devotee of the law and economics movement—a field based on the central insight that legal rules create behavioral incentives. Imagine telling, say, Richard Posner that we would suddenly make detention difficult and refuse for years to create a stable regime of known, clear rules. Imagine also that you had then asked this platonic Posner to identify the consequences. He probably would have replied that detention would grow less visible. We would release some people precipitously. We would rely on proxies more. We probably would kill some people that we might have captured before. Rarely does life comport with theory as well as detention policy has conformed to the predictions that law and economics would suggest. As the real Richard Posner wrote of the original decision to judicialize Guantánamo proceedings, it "seems like a sensible, 'practical' decision, but may not be. . . . [T]he decision may just encourage the government to hold more detainees abroad, say, in Afghanistan or Iraq, . . . and what would be gained by that?"[8]

None of what has happened was hard to predict. Water finds a path to the sea. Dam a river and it will flow around the dam. This metaphor, something of a cliché in discussing campaign finance law and attempts to regulate money in politics, applies with equal force in counterterrorism operations. The reason is simple, and we ignore it at considerable risk of intellectual blindness: The call to prevent terrorist events is so compelling politically that just as gravity operates on water, it will operate on politicians and other officials responsible for security. It will operate so strongly that new restrictions in one area will merely shift government energies to other areas. Encumber the use of one power, and authorities will just use another; throw a wrench in that one, and they'll move on to something else. If prosecutions in federal court are too hard, you create incentives to use military commissions. If the commissions are too generous to the accused, detention without trial will see greater use. Make it too tough to use a particular form of detention and the government will shift to others. Make detention broadly problematic and you promote the use of proxies less fastidious than we are and the use of drones.

The government interests at stake are so powerful that the executive will deploy every lawful option available and will show enormous creativity in expanding the field of options—both by making novel legal arguments and by developing tactical innovations. The attempt to force counterterrorism operations to take place through conventional means of law enforcement will impede it and channel it to some degree. For the most part, however, it will redirect it to less visible, less attractive, and more violent exercises of government power.

We cannot reconcile the competing interests that our political system requires our detention system to satisfy simultaneously. We want to incapacitate people who threaten our security. We want to ensure that we do not lock up innocent people, and we want to make sure that we don't let dangerous people walk free. We therefore want our authorities to be held accountable for those detained and for decisions to release people from detention. We want a system that our own courts will uphold and our domestic politics will tolerate—which is to say that we want a system that will make us proud or at least not embarrass us to the point that it generates its own fragility. And we want detention not to be a persistent sore point in our relations with the rest of the world.

Realizing at some level that we cannot square this particular circle, we have learned that we can fake it to a certain degree. Through a variety of means, we can lower the profile of our detention system; by ostentatiously closing our highest-profile detention facility—or, at least, announcing its closure—we can keep our residual detentions remote and invisible to the federal courts, the press, and the international public alike.

But this arrangement will, I suspect, prove to be a deceptively unstable equilibrium, for it depends on contemporary circumstances that are not likely to persist indefinitely. The most important of those is that we are currently adding only a small number of captives to the system. And small numbers permit a great deal. As long as the numbers stay small, proxy detention in the theater of operations presents a viable option for a high percentage of cases. As long as the numbers stay small, the domestic criminal justice system can plausibly absorb and handle most of the relatively rare cases in which rendition or proxy detention is not a reliable alternative. And as long as the number of new detainees entering the U.S. detention system is a rounding error on the number of detainees leaving it—either through release or transfer to foreign custody—the newcomers can be hidden among the declining overall population. The American public and the world at large will continue to see a declining detainee population and are likely not to care that the aggregate number of detainees masks some new entrants into the system.

The trouble is that it seems unlikely that the numbers will remain small forever. Eventually—and eventually may come soon—the United States will have to deploy forces to some location in the world where it lacks a local partner with the capacity to conduct our detentions for us. What happens then?

Another potential source of instability in the current equilibrium is the judiciary. At present, U.S. federal courts have clearly established jurisdiction to hear habeas corpus lawsuits from Guantánamo, and the government is resisting claims that they also have jurisdiction over some suits from Bagram. So far, the government has prevailed on this point at the appellate court level, after losing in district court. But whether the federal courts ultimately determine that they have habeas jurisdiction over overseas detentions besides those at Guantánamo will greatly influence the vitality of a policy based on keeping detentions hidden by keeping them far away. Such a policy, after all, is more robust if the courts play along with the government's out-of-sight, out-of-mind policy fiction than if they play a game of hide-and seek with the military's detention facilities. Policymakers face one environment if the courts will tolerate a multi-tiered detention system in which criminal detention within the United States is layered on top of judicially supervised, law-of-war detention for the shrinking number of Guantánamo detainees and that is layered on top of judicial abstention from detention everywhere else. They face an altogether different environment if the courts intend, to one degree or another, to follow military detentions around the world. The latter approach—while probably more intellectually coherent than asserting jurisdiction at Guantánamo and nowhere else—would leave the military without one of its chief ways to obscure detention.

Finally, the policy's vitality rests on domestic and international acceptance of the transparent fiction that detention at sites more remote and less visible than Guantánamo somehow addresses the concerns that demanded Guantánamo's closure in the first place. The hypothesis that this acceptance will in the long run materialize is only a hypothesis. It assumes that our allies, and our domestic elites, are really so naive, so stupid, or so partisan that they will take a less hostile attitude toward U.S. detention when it's conducted at facilities not named Guantánamo Bay by presidents not named George W. Bush. I am uncertain of that assumption. It is certainly possible that the world will tolerate a good bit of detention under such circumstances, as long as detention is a policy in retreat, not a policy on the march. But that only returns us to the conditions outlined above, in which the number of detainees is declining and proxy powers are increasingly capable of handling a higher percentage of them. Political tolerance for the current U.S. approach may not survive an increasing number of detainees, particularly if they end up in direct U.S. custody.

In short, the current equilibrium is not likely to persist forever. Its fragility is a function of both its dependence on current circumstances and its own incoherence. It is less a policy than a set of arrangements made in the absence of a policy. And at the core of its incoherence is its attempt to deal with a complex policy problem in the absence of clear rules. Nobody knows today exactly when it is legal to detain the enemy in global counterterrorism operations, who counts as the enemy, what procedures the executive and the courts must follow in evaluating detention cases, and what rights and protections the detainees must receive in the process. All of this is in flux, with different answers proposed for different facilities, different legal regimes, and different detainees. Uncertainty is the only sure thing.

And how could it be otherwise under current law? The only guidance that Congress has given is a single spare paragraph that does not mention detention and that makes no attempt to consider—let alone weigh—the many competing security, justice, diplomatic, and legal considerations that have arisen in the tens of thousands of detention cases in the years since Congress enacted that paragraph. The president, the legislature has informed us,

> is authorized to use all necessary and appropriate force against those nations, organizations, or persons he determines planned, authorized, committed, or aided the terrorist attacks that occurred on September 11, 2001, or harbored such organizations or persons, in order to prevent any future acts of international terrorism against the United States by such nations, organizations or persons.[9]

Apart from its various attempts to preclude judicial review of detentions, this high-altitude authorization to use military force is more or less all that Congress has said. The irony is that human rights groups, the Bush administration, the Obama administration, and most of the Obama administration's conservative critics all seem to agree that these spare words—about whose meaning they disagree profoundly—form an adequate basis for U.S. detention policy.

2

The Mythology and Reality of Preventive Detention in the United States

It is an article of faith in our discourse on terrorism that preventive detention runs counter to American values and law. That meme has become standard among civil liberties and human rights groups and in a great deal of legal scholarship, which treats the past nine years of extra-criminal detention of terrorism suspects as an extraordinary aberration from a strong constitutional norm that holds that government locks up citizens only as criminal punishment, not because of mere fear of their future acts. According to this view, any formalized administrative detention regime would be a radical departure from that norm, an institutionalization in American law of the aberration that the detention practices of the Bush years represented.

The more careful commentators pause here and acknowledge an uncomfortable truth: that the rule in question seems to have some exceptions. But, they continue, those exceptions are narrow, limited deviations from a generally strong rule, tolerated only to accommodate truly exceptional circumstances.

I could quote hundreds of examples of this view, for it has become a standard talking point among human rights activists,

This chapter is adapted from "Preventive Detention in American Practice and Theory" (forthcoming in the *Harvard National Security Journal*), an article that I wrote with a remarkable young scholar named Adam Klein. The research discussed in this chapter, as well as some of the text, reflects his work as well as mine.

detainee advocates, and liberal commentators. I will satisfy myself, however, with a single, personal example, which illustrates both the full scope of the meme's content and the function that it plays in the current debate. In 2009, a colleague and I released a paper proposing a model law for certain detentions. The paper attracted considerable attention when National Public Radio reported that members of the new administration were studying it closely. In the flurry of coverage, one news outlet sought comment from New York University scholar David Golove, a prominent international law expert. "One of the core features of liberal democracy is precisely that preventive detention is not allowed," he told the *Washington Independent*. "The struggle for constitutional liberty is in many ways a struggle against preventive detention." He dismissed the model law—whose terms I summarize in chapter 5—as "treat[ing] that whole problem incredibly cavalierly." While the wartime detention model has "deep historical roots," he said, other forms of preventive detention in American law are "carved out exceptions based on very specific rationales. Every time we add a new one we're breaking down the whole idea that preventive detention is problematic in a liberal country."[1]

Notice in particular how Golove invokes the entire weight of the liberal tradition to delegitimize the discussion of a preventive detention law for terrorism and how he also insists that the exceptions to the strong rule that he cites against preventive detention are narrow. To the extent that this belief prevails, it completely paralyzes any discussion of the possibility of crafting new detention rules for new circumstances.

This sort of civic mythology has a problem beyond the political paralysis that it induces: it is wrong. Indeed, nearly every aspect of it is false. Preventive detention is not prohibited by U.S. law or especially frowned upon in tradition or in practice. The circumstances under which federal and state law authorize it are not isolated exceptions to a strong rule against it; they arise with relative frequency. The federal government and all fifty states have statutory preventive detention regimes that are frequently used, often with little social or legal controversy. The diverse statutes and regimes authorizing the preventive locking up of an individual not convicted of a crime to prevent that person from causing harm range widely in purpose and subject matter:

—Wartime detention powers cover not only lawful and unlawful enemy combatants but also the civilian nationals of countries against which the United States finds itself in a state of armed conflict.

—The Constitution's suspension clause specifically contemplates that Congress might in a crisis suspend normal constitutional presumptions concerning detention—a power that has been invoked several times in U.S. history.

—Detention authorities ancillary to the criminal justice system include both pretrial detention and the detention of material witnesses who are not facing criminal charges.

—U.S. immigration law permits the detention of aliens facing deportation and "arriving aliens" denied entry to the United States.

—State and federal laws permit the detention of seriously mentally ill individuals when they pose a danger to themselves or to the public at large as well as the detention of sex offenders who have already completed their criminal sentences.

—State and federal statutes provide broad authority to quarantine people who have communicable diseases.

—States and localities have a variety of protective custody powers permitting the detention of, among others, intoxicated individuals, alcoholics, drug addicts, homeless individuals, and pregnant drug users, often for their own protection.

The simple reality is that there exists no broad principle in American law proscribing preventive detention. Instead, American law eschews it except when legislatures and courts deem it necessary to prevent grave public harms. The law then tends to countenance detention unapologetically to the extent that it is necessary to prevent such harm.

It also is wrong to describe preventive detention powers in American law as narrowly crafted exceptions to some broad constitutional rule or to suggest that once legitimized in law, preventive detention powers will metastasize and swallow up liberal democracy. Many of these powers evolved from common law detention powers that were, in fact, significantly *broader* than the form that they now take. That point bears emphasis. U.S. preventive detention powers did not evolve as regrettable and therefore narrow byways diverging from the main road of criminal justice detention. Many of them predated the Bill of Rights and have coexisted with it for the entirety of the life of the country. The narrowing of those powers has tended to occur in response to abuses and concerns that the powers in question authorize more detention than is strictly necessary.

What's more, the evolution of the scope of preventive detention powers is far from unidirectional. Detention powers may expand or contract as public sentiment evolves concerning how much detention a given problem truly requires. The United States today, for example, sees dramatically less use of quarantine for contagious diseases and detention for mental illness than in decades past. Yet the detention of sexual predators is on the rise, as is the detention of those facing deportation, and the post–September 11 period saw a significant increase in the detention of material witnesses.

In practice, the test that American law seems to apply to assess the legitimacy of preventive detention schemes of all types is simple: is the detention in question really necessary, and does the detention scheme work in a way that minimizes the risk of erroneous deprivation of liberty? Those are the questions that we should be asking with respect to detention in terrorism cases.

To illustrate the basic compatibility of well-thought-out counterterrorism detention authorities with the U.S. constitutional tradition, it is useful to begin by demythologizing somewhat the larger subject of preventive detention in federal and state law.

Surveying the many areas in which our laws countenance locking people up for things that they might do rather than for things that they already have done yields a simple, striking insight: the tradition is actually quite flexible and broadly responsive to society's needs at any given time. It demands justification for, but does not dogmatically forbid, preventive detention. It asks for appropriate procedures, not for abstention. The tradition, as Justice Robert Jackson famously said of the Bill of Rights, is not a suicide pact.

One of the reasons that our current debate so stigmatizes preventive detention is that we tend to define it in ways that exclude its most routine manifestations in contemporary society. Preventive detention occurs every day *within the criminal justice system*, for example, yet people have a tendency to define such deprivations of liberty as categorically different from noncriminal preventive detentions. Similarly, while we routinely describe the detention of unlawful combatants in pejorative language, the preventive detention of soldiers as prisoners of war is utterly uncontroversial—and tends even to escape description as preventive detention in the first place. This move badly stacks the intellectual deck. It's a little like defining all killing performed by the state as something other than killing (collateral damage or wartime targeting, for example), and then concluding that the state has no power to kill.

For present purposes, think of preventive detention as including the involuntary holding of any person that the state undertakes in order to prevent some future harm without first convicting the person of a criminal offense. The harm can include damage to other individuals, to the state, or even to the person detained. The wartime powers of the military offer some of the most vivid examples of preventive detention authorized in American law, and because of their frequent application in the counterterrorism context, they are a good place to begin a brief survey of preventive detention in the real American tradition.

The power to capture and hold enemy combatants, the post–September 11 controversy over it notwithstanding, is not typically a subject of dispute. It encompasses both the prisoner of war (the fighter who complies with the requirements of the Third Geneva Convention) and the unlawful combatant (the fighter who does not). The soldier, the law presumes, will continue to engage in armed hostilities as long as his nation is in a state of war and makes it his duty to do so. This point's natural corollary is that once the nation (or non-state group) to which he owes allegiance ceases to be at war, his duty to make war ends and the preventive rationale for his detention evaporates with it.

Enemy combatant detention is as old as warfare, and wartime detention illustrates pointedly the tendency of detention authorities to narrow—not expand—over time. Historically, captives in warfare, including civilians, were enslaved, became the chattel of the victor, and could be killed at the whim or convenience of their captors. By medieval times, the code of chivalry required feudal knights to respect the lives of captured adversaries, but only those of noble status. Civilians did not qualify for any protection under the feudal code until the fourteenth century. Instead, captors derived economic value from prisoners of war by demanding a ransom for their release. Demands for ransom, which occur repeatedly in the *Iliad* as a feature of Greek practice in the Trojan War, were still common in the seventeenth century. As warfare advanced, the rules, including the rules for treatment of captured enemies, advanced with it, and they finally took their rough modern shape: soldiers who respect the rules of war are entitled to an honorable detention with a series of generous benefits spelled out in the Third Geneva Convention, decent conditions, and immunity from prosecution for their belligerent acts. By contrast, while the state may detain those who do not follow the rules of warfare, it is not obliged to grant them the benefits of POWs, nor must it grant them immunity against criminal prosecution for their acts of war.

The legal power to detain enemy combatants thus neatly illustrates several of the general currents running through preventive detention in American practice. First, that power is not so much an exception to a broad constitutional norm that condones detention only within the criminal justice system as it is a power that runs on a parallel track but operates according to its own rules, which evolved without reference to criminal law. Second, those rules have not functioned as a slippery slope down which narrow detention powers have slid over time, growing in scope and menacing civil liberties. To the contrary, broad authorities to capture, kill, and ransom prisoners have narrowed over centuries of refinement and focus today on detaining under humane and respectful conditions only those people whom it is necessary to detain and only for as long as detention remains necessary.

U.S. law does not stop at permitting the long-term detention of the enemy fighter. A lesser known authority, still in force, also authorizes the detention of civilian nationals of countries with which the United States is at war. This power, like the power to detain enemy combatants, is overtly preventive in nature and not especially discriminating. Like the power to detain combatants, it evolved from far broader powers to take prisoners in wartime. Current federal law authorizes the president to detain an alien when "a declared war between the United States and any foreign nation or government" exists or when an "invasion or predatory incursion [is] attempted, or threatened against the territory of the United States by any foreign nation or government." The detainees must be "natives, citizens, denizens, or subjects of the hostile nation or government, being of the age of fourteen years and upward." The terms of the statute require no individualized determination of dangerousness or threat. Merely by being from a particular country, such individuals are "liable to be apprehended, restrained, secured, and removed as alien enemies."[2]

The alien enemy detention authority has a rather disreputable origin. It was first enacted in 1798 along with three other statutes, known collectively as the Alien and Sedition Acts, which together constitute the great historical stain on the administration of John Adams because of the prosecution under the Sedition Act of criticism of him or his administration. Yet unlike the Sedition Act, which expired in 1801, the alien enemy law has endured. While a 1918 amendment struck out language restricting its application to males only, Congress has otherwise left it intact. It also has seen a great deal of use, and it has survived judicial challenge. James Madison detained British citizens under it during the War of 1812. On February 23, 1813, the State Department issued an order by which, as a court later summarized, "alien enemies, residing within forty miles of tide water" were required "to retire to such places beyond that distance from tide water as should be designated" by federal marshals, who were authorized to arrest those who did not comply with the order.[3]

Similarly, in World War I, thousands of enemy aliens were interned under the act. On April 6, 1917, President Woodrow Wilson issued a proclamation invoking the statute with regard to German citizens in the United States. The proclamation established rules restricting the conduct of German aliens and provided that any who violated any regulation—"or of whom there is reasonable ground to believe that he is about to violate, any regulation duly promulgated by the President"—was "subject to summary arrest . . . and to confinement."[4] Subsequent regulations required enemy aliens to register and carry their registration card on their persons at all times.[5] After Congress amended the statute in 1918 to apply to women as well as men, Wilson issued another proclamation requiring female enemy aliens to comply with the regulations.[6]

Following the Japanese attack on Pearl Harbor, the Roosevelt administration immediately invoked the act once again. On December 8, 1941, Roosevelt issued proclamations as required under the statute regarding German, Japanese, and Italian enemy aliens.[7] According to a 1943 account in the *American Journal of International Law,* "within six weeks after the attack on Pearl Harbor, 3,138 alien enemies had been apprehended, including 1,309 Germans, 243 Italians, and 1,581 Japanese." By the end of

the first year of U.S. involvement in the war, the number apprehended had grown to 12,071. Of those, only 3,646 were ultimately
interned long term.[8] Those detentions, it bears emphasizing, were
separate from the infamous internment of Pacific Coast Japanese
and Japanese Americans. Those internments were not conducted
pursuant to the enemy alien authorities, which could not have
justified the holding of U.S. citizens, but under an executive order.

The World War II era also saw direct Supreme Court consideration of the constitutionality of the Alien Enemies Act, in a 1948
case, *Ludecke* v. *Watkins*. In an opinion by Justice Felix Frank-
furter, the Court upheld the removal of a German citizen under a
proclamation issued under the act, even though that removal took
place after the cessation of hostilities. The Court held that the act
did not permit judicial review of the president's actions within the
broad discretionary power that it granted him. It also rejected the
claim that the power expired with active hostilities, noting that
"power to be exercised by the President such as that conferred by
the Act of 1798 is a process which begins when war is declared
but is not exhausted when the shooting stops." The Court went
on to uphold the constitutionality of the act against a due process
claim: "The Act is almost as old as the Constitution, and it would
savor of doctrinaire audacity now to find the statute offensive to
some emanation of the Bill of Rights."[9]

Again, the Alien Enemies Act is best understood as a narrowed
variant of an age-old wartime power to capture the civilians of
the other side. It was once the norm to enslave such people. Over
time enslavement gave way to detention, and as the laws of war
were codified, civilized countries began to ensure that civilians
had some protections. Today, it is international law more than
U.S. constitutional or statutory law that constrains the detention
of enemy aliens. The Fourth Geneva Convention provides various legal rights for "protected persons," which generally includes
foreign nationals in the territory of a belligerent power. The convention forbids detention except "if the security of the Detaining

Power makes it absolutely necessary."[10] In short, like the power to detain enemy soldiers, the power to detain enemy civilians was not carved out as an exception to criminal justice norms but evolved in parallel from a far broader authority that has narrowed considerably over time.

The Constitution also contains its own express contemplation of wartime suspension of the constitutional norms that would otherwise limit executive detention. "The privilege of the writ of habeas corpus shall not be suspended," it says, "unless when in cases of rebellion or invasion the public safety may require it."[11] The so-called suspension clause is not itself a preventive detention authority but a kind of permission within the Constitution to designate certain circumstances in which preventive executive detentions may occur without habeas review. It thus foresees the possibility of detentions that it would not otherwise tolerate. Executive detention under suspension of habeas corpus is the modern descendant of the royal authority to detain subjects as necessary to maintain the peace of the realm. U.S. law has banished that power almost entirely, but not quite. It quite consciously reserved that portion of it that the Framers deemed necessary: a carve-out from the usual rules for the worst of times. And occasionally throughout U.S. history, authorities have invoked it more or less in that spirit.

The history of its invocation began even before the Constitution was written. In 1786, the outbreak of Shays' Rebellion in western Massachusetts prompted an act to suspend the privilege of the writ of habeas corpus. Barely two decades later, the alleged Aaron Burr conspiracy prompted President Jefferson to seek legislation in 1807 to suspend the writ so that he could suppress the alleged plot, but Congress voted down the bill. Abraham Lincoln famously suspended habeas corpus during the Civil War, both on his own dubious constitutional authority and later with the blessing of Congress. And in the war's wake, during Reconstruction,

Congress again authorized the president to suspend the writ in order to suppress the Ku Klux Klan in the South.[12]

Congress also authorized the suspension of the writ in 1902 in establishing a temporary civil government for the Philippines and suspended it again a few years later to control gangs of bandits.[13] And similarly, the 1900 law establishing jurisdiction over Hawaii gave the governor the power to suspend the writ "until communication can be had with the President and his decision thereon made known."[14] That provision was invoked and the writ suspended by the governor on December 7, 1941, immediately after the Japanese attack on Pearl Harbor. The president then approved the action on December 9.[15]

To summarize the matter bluntly, U.S. law grants the president a variety of preventive detention powers in wartime and, in addition, creates a stopgap measure through which he can—with Congress's approval—disregard virtually all other restraints on detention. In theoretical terms, those powers cover the counterterrorism arena relatively comfortably. The United States, after all, is at war, as all three branches of the government clearly acknowledge. The problem in the counterterrorism arena is not the absence of adequately broad detention powers. It is instead the absence of authorities tailored to the specific circumstances that the country faces, which involve a conflict with no conceptually identifiable endpoint and the capture of large numbers of people who are hard to identify in situations in which their affiliation with the enemy, if any, is difficult to determine. The military's preventive detention powers are so broad that when applied to that group of people, they engender judicial and public discomfort—which triggers in turn the narrowing of those powers in unpredictable ways.

The criminal justice system itself contains two major preventive detention powers. As noted, analysts often succumb to the temptation to ignore both pretrial detention of people charged with a crime and the holding of material witnesses as somehow not counting as preventive detention. They take place, after all, within the four corners of the larger criminal law apparatus, a system that represents the hallmark of legitimacy. But this intellectual sleight of hand is a mistake. Those powers involve the authority to lock up people who, even when indicted, are supposed to benefit from a presumption of innocence. Such detentions take place for overtly preventive, nonpunitive reasons—either to protect the community or to prevent the flight of individuals who are charged with a crime or whose testimony the government needs. In addition, they take place in the face of an explicit constitutional prohibition against excessive bail. Despite the constitutional promise of speedy trial, pretrial detention can persist for astonishingly long periods of time. Again, the law tolerates this system because it deems it necessary.

The modern federal pretrial detention framework was codified by the Bail Reform Act of 1984, whose most notable feature for present purposes was its creation of a detention option based on danger to "any other person or the community"—something that had not existed previously.[16] Previously, the legal system had regarded securing the attendance of the accused in court as the sole permissible objective of imposing bail, and judges had tended to address public safety concerns sub rosa in setting bail amounts. The new law gave them explicit permission to deny bail on the basis of the perceived dangerousness of the accused. Civil liberties groups, including the American Civil Liberties Union, opposed the 1984 reform as a violation of the presumption of innocence, but the Supreme Court upheld its constitutionality. In its current form, the law authorizes a judicial officer to order pretrial detention if he "finds that no condition or combination of conditions" will reasonably ensure both the appearance of the person at trial as required *and* the safety of other persons or the community.[17]

Preventive detention under the Bail Reform Act is extraordinarily pervasive, involving a significant percentage of the tens of thousands of people charged with federal crimes. States too permit pretrial detention in certain circumstances. Some states have laws or constitutional provisions allowing pretrial detention along the lines of the federal statute or have a right to bail except in capital cases or some specified subset of very serious felonies. Some states do not leave the determination of "dangerousness" to judges but permit certain categories of offenders to be denied bail. A 2008 Bureau of Justice Statistics report on pretrial detention in the largest urban areas in the United States reveals just how prevalent state pretrial detention is: 43 percent of those charged with felony offenses and 88 percent of those charged with murder were detained until case disposition.[18]

U.S. criminal law does not even require that one be charged with a crime to face detention within the criminal justice system; it also authorizes the detention of material witnesses. Detention of witnesses dates from the beginning of our constitutional system. The Judiciary Act of 1789 provided for the authority to detain witnesses, which traditionally was quite broad.[19] The power went through various iterations over the nation's life, but detention took place commonly and largely without controversy before September 11. For example, Human Rights Watch reports that the federal government made 4,168 material witness arrests in 2000—overwhelmingly by immigration officials.[20]

But the material witness statute has also found use in high-profile criminal and terrorist cases. Two days after the Oklahoma City bombing, a federal district court in Oklahoma issued a material witness warrant for the arrest of Terry Lynn Nichols. Only later, when Nichols's involvement in the bombing had become apparent to investigators, did authorities issue an arrest warrant based on a criminal complaint. In its investigations following the September 11 attacks, the FBI used material witness warrants to detain dozens of persons suspected of having a connection to the hijackers. The FBI acknowledges that its material witness arrests increased by 80 percent from 2000 to 2002, but it has not given a specific number. Human Rights Watch asserts that the material witness statute was used to detain at least seventy people in the investigations, only seven of whom were eventually charged with a terrorism-related crime.[21]

The current material witness law provides that if "the testimony of a person is material in a criminal proceeding, and if it is shown that it may become impracticable to secure the presence of the person by subpoena, a judicial officer may order the arrest of the person." The order can be issued only when the judicial officer "finds that no condition or combination of conditions will reasonably assure the appearance of the person as required." Moreover, detention of the witness is limited to "a reasonable period of time until the deposition of the witness can be taken."[22] In other words, the statute is carefully crafted to make sure that it does not authorize more detention than is strictly necessary. Nearly every state has some material witness law to complement the federal authority.

Then there are the immigration powers. No preventive detention regime in American law sees as much use or affects as many people as does the immigration detention system. On an average day, says Homeland Security Secretary Janet Napolitano, "roughly 33,400 detainees are housed under ICE authority at as many as 350 detention facilities nationwide."[23] Those people are not serving time for criminal convictions; they are locked up to prevent them from entering and moving freely within the United States, to prevent them from committing crimes in the United States, to prevent them from fleeing deportation proceedings, or to prevent them from engaging in terrorist activity. Immigration detention has risen dramatically in recent years.

Preventive detention under the Immigration and Naturalization Act is multifaceted and has several distinct purposes. The first broad category of detainable aliens includes those deemed inadmissible on arrival in the United States. Generally speaking, arriving aliens are to be detained pending deportation proceedings unless they are "clearly and beyond a doubt entitled to be admitted."[24] This general rule has certain humanitarian exceptions, the most important being that aliens detained under its terms may be paroled into the United States. The result is that a large number of people may be residing in the United States at any given time who have never been legally admitted.

The second broad category involves aliens legally admitted to the United States who are awaiting deportation proceedings. Generally, aliens in the United States may "be arrested and detained pending" deportation proceedings.[25] The government may release such aliens on bail or on conditional parole, or it may continue to detain them. In other words, anyone facing deportation proceedings may find himself in custody until he is deported. Detention is mandatory for criminal aliens and for those suspected of terrorism.

The third category involves noncitizens for whom a final removal order has been issued who have not yet been deported. Current law generally requires detention of an alien ordered to be removed pending deportation.

The dramatic broadening in law and practice of immigration detention has ironically coincided with something of a conceptual narrowing of detention powers and the application to them of stricter due process norms. As late as the 1950s, the Supreme Court showed little anxiety about indefinite immigration detention without substantial legal process. More recently, however, the Court has taken a stricter view. In a pair of cases in 2001 and 2005, it interpreted the authority to detain deportable and inadmissible aliens narrowly to no longer authorize detention once there is no longer any prospect of actually removing the prospective deportee, and it slapped a presumptive six-month limit on detention pending removal.[26] But while the Court has begun reading time limits into immigration detention statutes, it has remained solicitous of the propriety of detention itself. That means, in short, that immigration detention remains viable as long as it is not permanent and it is reasonably tied to the purpose of the underlying proceedings: to remove people from the country who are not entitled to live in it.

State legal authorities concerning public health present in some respects the paradigmatic case of legal preventive detention. They not only permit the detention of people in the absence of criminal charges, they even in certain instances authorize detention of a person whose mental health poses a menace to the public following his or her completion of a sentence pursuant to a criminal conviction. These authorities evolved from broader common law authorities as the public perception of the necessity of such detentions narrowed, and over time courts and legislatures have invested them with increasing procedural protections in response to abuses. In general, mental health authorities have evolved further in this direction than has the power of quarantine—both because the latter has seen so little use in the modern era and because the symptoms associated with communicable diseases and the dangers of contagion are easier to establish authoritatively. But the broad pattern is similar, and it bears little resemblance to the mythological pattern of narrow exceptions to a broad criminal justice norm.

While federal law provides for the detention of mentally ill persons in some circumstances, health detention authorities are principally a state affair. Their origins, like those of the military's detention authorities, are very old. An English law of 1714 provided justices of the peace with authority to "Apprehend[] and [keep] safely Locked up" persons "of little or no Estates, who, by Lunacy . . . are furiously Mad, and dangerous to be permitted to go Abroad."[27] The colonies inherited that tradition, and the new states incorporated it. In 1788, for example, New York state enacted a law providing that "persons who by lunacy or otherwise are furiously mad, or are so far disordered in their senses that they may be dangerous to be permitted to go abroad" could be held "in some secure place, and, if . . . necessary, to be there chained."[28] A Massachusetts statute dealing with "Rogues,

Vagabonds, Common Beggars and other idle, disorderly and lewd Persons" made similar provisions.[29]

For most of the life of the country, detention of the mentally ill took place under permissive legal standards. That began to change in the 1960s in response to abuses—both needless deprivations of liberty and abuses of people in confinement. In a series of cases, the Supreme Court narrowed the circumstances in which it tolerated civil commitment, and it required state civil commitment procedures to include a number of due process protections.

As a result of that reorientation, states may not commit a person merely because he or she is mentally ill. Detention requires a finding of mental illness *and* a finding that the person presents a danger—either an imminent danger or, depending on the jurisdiction, one in the foreseeable future—to himself or to others. In some jurisdictions, in lieu of a dangerousness finding, a court can authorize detention when a person requires treatment and is incapable of caring for himself. In either case, confinement is authorized only as long as the mental illness or dangerousness persists, and the necessity of continuing to detain a person is subject to periodic review. Many states require that authorities consider less-restrictive alternatives before seeking involuntary commitment.

States also may detain persons acquitted of crimes by reason of insanity or found incompetent to stand trial. A finding of not guilty by reason of insanity, after all, establishes both conduct constituting a criminal act and a mental illness. The state may hold the acquitted defendant until he or she ceases to satisfy one of the two conditions—mental illness or dangerousness—even if the term of confinement runs beyond the length of the maximum allowable prison term for the offense.

An important variant of the civil commitment of the mentally ill involves the commitment of violent sexual predators, even after they have completed lengthy prison sentences. Commitment statutes specifically targeting "sexual psychopaths" were first passed in the 1930s, an era in which pedophilia was considered a mental disorder rendering offenders unable to control their deviant impulses. Those statutes fell out of favor in the 1970s and 1980s as policymakers increasingly focused on criminal punishment.

In recent years, however, the statutes have made something of a comeback. In 1990, Washington state initiated the current era of violent sexual predator laws by passing the first modern version of earlier statutes. The act provides for civil commitment of "sexually violent predators" at the end of their criminal sentences. It requires a judge or jury to find beyond a reasonable doubt that an inmate is a sexually violent predator, defined as "any person who has been convicted of or charged with a crime of sexual violence and who suffers from a mental abnormality or personality disorder which makes the person likely to engage in predatory acts of sexual violence if not confined in a secure facility."[30] Many other states followed suit, and the Supreme Court in 1997 upheld Kansas's law.[31] As of 2007, approximately 2,700 convicted sex offenders were being held under civil commitment authorities in the United States of the 3,000 offenders who have been committed nationwide since the Washington state law was passed in 1990.[32] Those figures suggest a low rate of release from commitment.

Federal law too permits civil commitment of dangerous sexual predators. In 2006, Congress passed a federal civil commitment regime for inmates in the Bureau of Prisons—or persons charged with federal crimes who are found to lack capacity to stand trial—who may be "sexually dangerous persons." The statute defines a "sexually dangerous person" as "a person who has engaged or attempted to engage in sexually violent conduct or child molestation and . . . suffers from a serious mental illness, abnormality, or disorder as a result of which he would have serious difficulty in refraining from sexually violent conduct or child molestation if released." A person deemed a "sexually dangerous person" in a hearing is committed to the custody of the attorney general, who can then either pawn him off on a state government or "place the person for treatment in a suitable facility" until a state assumes custody of him or until he no longer meets the requirements for detention.[33] The Supreme Court in 2010 upheld the statute against a constitutional challenge.[34]

Sex offender detention statutes offer an interesting contrast with more traditional commitment laws. As a practical matter, their evidentiary threshold is higher, since the underlying criminal conviction operates to ensure that people are not detained without proof beyond a reasonable doubt of criminal conduct. On the other hand, the detentions can in theory be quite indefinite, and judging from the number of individuals released, much of the time they seem to operate that way in practice. Moreover, because detention follows the completion of a sentence based on a criminal conviction, it smacks painfully of incarcerating people twice for the same conduct. And the fact that the additional time is predicated on a "mental abnormality" that may or may not correspond to a known mental illness means that the detention criteria come uncomfortably close to defining such an abnormality as having committed one sex crime and having a propensity to commit others.

Detention powers in the health arena are not limited to mental illnesses. Although the power of quarantine and isolation for communicable diseases does not see a great deal of use today, it is one of the most powerful rebuttals of the notion that American law does not condone detention without extensive due process protections or at least the imputation of wrongdoing. Broad powers to lock people up for the simple reason that they are sick and potentially contagious have coexisted comfortably with the criminal justice system since long before the dawn of the United States. Those authorities remain broad today. Perhaps because their use has declined over the years, their sweep has remained potent, and they have seen only modest abridgment as a result of the due process revolution that has cabined other preventive authorities.

They represent an almost pure case of necessity driving the scope of detention powers. In fact, the case law says quite directly that, in this area, what is necessary bounds what is lawful.

Human societies have isolated and ostracized diseased individuals since the dawn of communal life. The American colonies had quarantine laws long before they became states. Those laws have been used aggressively at times, particularly in periods before the advent of antibiotics and widespread vaccination. As public health measures improved, the use of the laws tapered off dramatically. That said, they remain available for use—a reserve of considerable state power. And the scares over SARS and swine flu have raised the possibility of their renewed use on broad scale. Insofar as the courts have considered isolation and quarantine, they have allowed those measures to the detriment of an individual's personal liberty to the extent that they are reasonably necessary to preserve public health and safety.

The case law on quarantine is relatively sparse, but the courts have generally tolerated it and imposed few due process requirements. Today, both state and federal authorities authorize isolation and quarantine. The most commonly used isolation laws these days are tuberculosis control statutes that authorize the detention of recalcitrant carriers, whose refusal to comply with a mandated course of treatment can spread the disease and create drug-resistant strains. Most states have TB control statutes specifically authorizing public health officials to isolate carriers in their homes or in hospitals under such circumstances. The authority to restrain the person lasts until he or she is no longer infectious or otherwise ceases to be a danger to the public health—for example, by voluntarily complying with his or her treatment regime. And just as the courts a century ago tolerated detention to prevent the spread of typhoid, the courts today are tolerating tuberculosis detentions, limiting them largely by insisting that officials demonstrate their necessity.

A final, little-discussed category of detention authority involves situations in which the state acts to protect the detained individual from his or her own behavior. The exercise of this power is subject to two limitations: the individual must be incapable of making rational decisions, and the power must be exercised in the best interests of that individual. Some of these powers are best understood as a subset of the health authorities described above. Others, however, are distinct in that they do not merely protect the larger society from the consequences of the detainee's physical or mental illness but ensure that the detainee receives care that he or she might not otherwise get.

Several states, for example, still have laws authorizing mandatory treatment for substance abuse and permit some measure of civil commitment to facilitate treatment. California, to cite one, has long authorized the civil commitment of drug addicts not convicted of a crime. Any person who "is addicted to the use of narcotics or by reason of the repeated use of narcotics is in imminent danger of becoming addicted to their use" may be civilly committed and confined in a "narcotic detention, treatment and rehabilitation facility" on petition by the district attorney.[35] While the Supreme Court has never confronted one of these statutes directly and they do not appear to see much use these days, it has indicated strongly that they are constitutionally acceptable. In a 1962 case the justices held unconstitutional a California law that criminalized "be[ing] addicted to the use of narcotics," but the majority specifically noted that "a State might establish a program of compulsory treatment for those addicted to narcotics [that] might require periods of involuntary confinement."[36]

Many states similarly permit the involuntary commitment of alcoholics. For example, Washington state includes both alcoholism and drugs in its definition of "chemical dependency" and, like California, authorizes compulsory residential treatment in some instances.[37] Other states subsume drug and alcohol addiction under the general category of "mental illness" for purposes of civil commitment.

One interesting subset of alcoholic statutes permits officers to civilly commit, on a temporary emergency basis, intoxicated persons whom they encounter in the course of their duties—in essence providing them with time to "dry out" before sending them back into society. Such statutes may reflect a preference for preventive civil detention rather than criminal prosecution. For example, a Colorado statute bars any political subdivision of the state from "adopt[ing] or enforc[ing] a local law, ordinance, resolution, or rule having the force of law that [criminalizes] drinking, being a common drunkard, or being found in an intoxicated condition."[38] It requires that when "any person is intoxicated or incapacitated by alcohol and clearly dangerous to the health and safety of himself, herself, or others, such person shall be taken into protective custody by law enforcement authorities or an emergency service patrol . . . only for so long as may be necessary to prevent injury to himself, herself, or others or to prevent a breach of the peace."[39]

This active preference for preventive civil detention as a more liberal alternative to criminal prosecution turns the tables on one of the most prevalent tropes about the preventive detention of terrorists—namely, that criminal prosecution and the lengthy prison sentences that it often imposes better respect the human and civil rights of terrorism suspects. In fact, in at least some areas, American law regards preventive detention as the more humane manner for preventing harm to society and its individual members.

Protective custody has other iterations as well. For example, several states have noncriminal statutes that specifically permit the civil commitment of pregnant women whose alcohol or drug use endangers the life or health of their unborn children. Not all protective custody arrangements concern themselves with the protection of the larger society; some reflect a simple paternalistic interest in the individual. When the weather drops below

32 degrees Fahrenheit, the New York City Department of Homeless Services arranges for the "involuntary transport" of at-risk homeless persons to shelters.[40] A similar program exists in Philadelphia.[41] Such programs are designed simply to protect the individuals in question—whether they want that protection or not—using detention to achieve that end.

There is, in short, no broad prohibition of preventive detention in American law. The pattern that emerges from a survey of the array of laws that authorize detention is simply not consistent with the civic mythology that American law abhors the practice or tolerates it only as a narrow exception in extreme situations. Nor is it consistent with the assertion that detention authorities have a tendency to metastasize to the detriment of liberty. The actual place of preventive detention in American law is rather more prosaic: Congress and state legislatures create preventive detention authorities without apology when they deem them necessary, and the courts uphold them when judges agree with legislators' judgment. These authorities sometimes expand; they also often tend to contract over time. The test of necessity, stripping away the doctrinal specificity that applies in any individual area, is relatively simple: First, how dire are the potential consequences of a failure to detain? And second, is the detention structured in a fashion that minimizes the possibility of error?

All of which makes the deep anxiety and shame that we seem to harbor about preventive detention in the counterterrorism arena a bit puzzling. Why should a society that tolerates without much discussion—let alone soul-searching—the preventive detention of pregnant drug users in the interests of fetal protection blanch at the detention of a suspected terrorist who aims to kill, among many other people, pregnant women and their fetuses? Why should a society that tolerates the detentions of tens of thousands of economic migrants who pose only the danger of flight and of working illegally in this country develop special scruples about the detention of sworn military enemies of the country against whom Congress has specifically authorized the use of deadly force?

Ironically, the insistence that preventive detention is presumptively off limits except in the most extreme circumstances tends to obscure the far more powerful argument against the creation of new preventive powers in the national security arena: that the normal rules that seem to govern preventive detention will not apply in these high-stakes cases. One might reasonably imagine that national security–based detentions will prove unusually subject to abuse as well as to exaggerated assessments of necessity and detainee dangerousness and to public hysteria. Precisely because water will find its way to the sea, national security detentions will find their way around whatever reasonable rules are put in place to govern them. This argument is different from and far more challenging than the straight-up objections to preventive detention in the counterterrorism context, but the advocate of candor seldom finds himself addressing it. In any event, the answer to it is relatively simple. First, the real choice is not between honestly facing our detention policy choices and not doing any national security detentions. As I have shown, it is a choice between honestly facing our detention policy needs and *not* facing those needs but creating elaborate mechanisms for obfuscating the detention in which we engage anyway. The latter choice seems far more prone to abuse than setting out clear rules to govern our behavior.

The simple reality is that preventive detention of suspected terrorists, assuming for a moment that it is truly necessary and tailored to encompass only those who pose a genuine danger, fits relatively comfortably in conceptual terms alongside other detention authorities. Much as the post-conviction detention of the sexual predator evolved as a specialized example of the broader detention of the dangerously mentally ill, the detention of terrorist suspects is evolving as a specialized case of the broader category of detention of unlawful combatants. Like detentions in the broader category, these detentions involve people associated with the enemy in military conflicts, and their purpose is to incapacitate enemy forces by means short of killing.

A plurality of the Supreme Court has described "detention to prevent a combatant's return to the battlefield" in the current conflict as "a fundamental incident of waging war"—implying acceptance of its necessity.[42] Both of the political branches of government have concurred. Congress has both tacitly and actively supported detention operations, and the executive branch, under both the Bush and Obama administrations, has insisted on the propriety of noncriminal military detention in counterterrorism cases. While human rights groups, detainees' lawyers, and academics have repeatedly questioned the necessity of preventive detention of suspected terrorists, no branch of government has done so.

Yet the evolution of this category of detention has also followed the broader pattern of a narrowing of authority to ensure the accuracy of detention decisions. The Supreme Court in *Boumediene* grafted habeas corpus review onto the Guantánamo detentions, adding robust adversarial judicial processes to military detentions that the courts traditionally had not supervised.[43] Military detainees, or at least those at Guantánamo, get access to counsel. At least for now, the burden of proof lies with the government, and the government has lost a majority of the habeas cases that have gone to decision. The due process norms that are developing in this area are quite elaborate—and so are those in most of the proposals for statutory administrative detention schemes. In other words, terrorism-related detention is both evolving out of a broader detention authority because of perceived necessity and developing more rigorous due process protections at the same time to guarantee that the government does not authorize more detention than society truly needs. It is, in short, following the broader pattern relatively neatly.

Except in one respect. In none of the other areas has shame induced denial or inhibited candor to the extent that it has in counterterrorism cases. In almost every other area discussed here,

I have described statutory or treaty law that overtly contemplates the detention in question. Detention takes place in the open; its parameters are debated by the relevant polities, defined in law, and refined by legislatures and courts. In none of the other areas have we displayed the kind of collective cowardice that we are now displaying as a political culture with respect to counter-terrorism—creating a layer cake of obfuscation to convince the world, and ourselves, that we are not detaining people. In none of those areas are we actively choosing less humane detention conditions—or even killing people—to avoid being candid about the nature of our project. The very thought, for example, of turning mentally ill individuals over to third world mental institutions so that we do not have to sully our hands with civil commitment is comical in its moral abhorrence. Such an approach should be no less abhorrent when the detainee is evil instead of sick.

3

The Emerging
Law of Detention

Its serial failures of candor with respect to detention unfortunately cannot relieve the United States of the burden of detention. Consequently, they also will not relieve it of the need for various systems of rules, norms, and procedures to handle the various types of people that U.S. forces and their proxies will end up capturing. The political system's refusal to engage seriously over the question simply delegates the foundational decisions regarding the contours of those systems to other actors.

We should face squarely who those actors are. When the United States turns tens of thousands of detainees over to the Iraqi and Afghan governments, it delegates to those countries the power to define the permissible boundaries of U.S. national security detentions. It relinquishes control over the conditions of confinement, and it also relinquishes control over the criteria for release. There are many excellent reasons to cede authority over time to those governments; they will, after all, eventually have to take responsibility for their own affairs. Fear of defining the rules ourselves, however, is not one of those excellent reasons.

This chapter is adapted from "The Emerging Law of Detention: The Guantánamo Habeas Cases as Lawmaking," a paper that I published with Robert Chesney and Rabea Benhalim on the Brookings Institution website in January 2010. Much of the research and some of the text reflect their work. The original paper is available at www.brookings.edu/~/media/Files/rc/papers/2010/0122_guantanamo_wittes_chesney/0122_guantanamo_wittes_chesney.pdf.

Closer to home, at Guantánamo, our refusal to take responsibility for designing a detention system empowers a different body: the U.S. courts. As discussed previously, the decision not to seek a legislatively defined detention regime does not mean that the Obama administration has abandoned the option of noncriminal detention of terrorist suspects. To the contrary, the administration specifically intends to continue holding around fifty suspects without trial, and that number does not include dozens of Yemeni suspects whom it would repatriate either immediately or eventually were it not for the ban on repatriations to Yemen that it has slapped on itself. Like the fifty other suspects, those people aren't going anywhere anytime soon.

Nor does the decision not to seek legislation mean that there exists no process to define the rules governing detentions. What the decision does mean is that for good or ill, the rules will be written by judges through the common-law process of litigating the habeas corpus cases of the detainees still held at Guantánamo.

This state of affairs puts a premium on the Guantánamo habeas cases not merely as a means of deciding the fate of the individuals in question but as a lawmaking exercise with broad implications for the future. The law established in these cases will in all likelihood govern not merely the Guantánamo detentions but also any other detentions around the world over which U.S. courts eventually acquire habeas jurisdiction. And while the courts currently seem to have little appetite for habeas beyond Guantánamo, that may not last indefinitely. What's more, to the extent that these cases establish substantive and procedural rules governing the application of law-of-war detention powers in general, they could end up affecting detentions far beyond those immediately supervised by the federal courts. After all, when the federal courts proclaim that the Authorization for Use of Military Force (AUMF) authorizes detention in situation X but not in situation Y, that rule of law presumably defines the government's authority whether or not the detainee in question has access to habeas courts. Presumably that rule must guide detention operations that aspire to remain within the law whether or not habeas judges are looking over the shoulders of military lawyers.

University of Texas legal scholar Robert Chesney has aptly dubbed this effect the "Mark Martins Problem." General Mark Martins took over detention operations at Bagram after helping to run the Obama administration's detention policy task force. In considering a habeas opinion or a judicial approach to a particular problem, Chesney—who also served on the task force—often poses the question of what message it would send to Martins and the people that he commands. Does it help to clarify their task or make matters murkier? Does it make their job easier or harder? Does it give them healthier or less healthy incentives? Are the courts sending consistent messages or mixed ones?

The implications of the Guantánamo habeas cases don't end with the Martins problem. The cases might have an impact on superficially unrelated military activities such as operations planning and decisionmaking regarding whether to target an individual with lethal force. To the extent that these cases interpret the AUMF's substantive authority to detain the enemy, they also necessarily interpret the scope of the substantive authority to target the enemy or, more generally, to wage war on the enemy. The task of deciding against whom Congress has authorized the use of "all necessary and appropriate force" only secondarily concerns itself with the power to lock someone up. Primarily, it concerns the power to blow someone up, and rules that declare certain people outside the scope of the AUMF for detention purposes necessarily raise questions about who lies within its scope for targeting purposes—and how, in the absence of extensive judicial process, one can tell whether someone lies within or beyond its scope for purposes of targeting.

The Guantánamo cases also offer an interesting study in the manner in which rules emerge in the absence of leadership. In these cases, they have emerged because the executive branch refused over a long period of time to engage the legislature in defining the rules, and the result has been that a diffuse set of actors have been groping their way toward rules in the absence of clear guidance and in the face of the need to decide large numbers of individual cases. The oddity of this particular manner of deciding national security policy makes it well worth pausing over the courts' work to date and mapping the contours of the nascent law of noncriminal counterterrorism detention that is emerging from it. This body of law doesn't look much like the law that a sensible political system would design. Indeed, I would suggest that it serves the key interests of neither the detainees nor the government.

Lawyers for the detainees have advocated relentlessly for habeas review as the appropriate adjudication mechanism and have fiercely opposed any alternative. Yet the emerging system consistently fails to give the detainees what they really need from a system of review. For the detainees, after all, speed is of the essence. The innocent detainee rounded up by mistake has an abiding interest in getting before whatever adjudication mechanism there is relatively quickly and having a chance to make his case in a reasonable period of time. Under the current system, Guantánamo detainees have waited years; even after *Boumediene*, only a minority had seen their cases go to resolution as of the summer of 2010. In all but a few of the hundreds of instances in which the government has released detainees, the releases preceded rather than followed adjudication of the cases. The system, in other words, certainly puts pressure on the government to resolve detainee cases in general, but adjudications are not functioning quickly enough to matter to the vast majority of individual detainees.

It also is in the interest of detainees to have a review mechanism governing their cases that is consistent across the various detention facilities. To the detainee at Bagram who does not receive habeas review solely because the government chose to store him in Afghanistan rather than in Cuba, a system of full-blown habeas review for the more geographically fortunate must seem like the very definition of arbitrary government. Review rules that allow the government to opt out of the legal process by keeping new detainees out of Guantánamo—exactly what it has done now for the past several years—hardly serves the interests of detainees as a class.

Detainees also have an interest in regularity of review, which the current system does not provide even for Guantánamo detainees. Evidence in detention cases can change notably over time; circumstances can change too, as the policies and capacities of detainees' countries of origins shift. The release of dangerous Saudi detainees was once unthinkable, for example, but it became not merely plausible but desirable as the Saudi government developed programs to manage the reintegration of violent radicals into society. Ideally, therefore, from a given detainee's perspective, a finding that the detainee had been reasonably held in the first instance would not be the end of the matter but would instead be followed by regular revisiting of the evidence and the conclusion. Nothing of the kind takes place in the Guantánamo habeas process. Judges hear the initial case. They rule, and if they rule against the detainee and the judgment withstands appeal, future detention reverts to purely a matter of executive discretion—forever. Detainees get one bite at the apple, and that's it.

But to say that the habeas system disserves detainees is not to say that it serves the government's interests. Far from it. It is a lose-lose system, and the government is one of the biggest losers. The government, first and foremost, has an abiding interest in certainty and predictability—in having known standards. Officials can live under restrictive rules (at some cost, of course), but they need to know that a detention that they undertake today under standards that they think that they understand will stand up in court tomorrow. They need to know what they will have to prove, using what sort of procedures and what sort of evidence.

And they need to know that those standards will not change, leaving them accountable for following rules that they never imagined would govern their conduct.

Under current law, they get no such certainty. Indeed, military officials have found themselves caught up in a kind of bait-and-switch maneuver in which they took detainees into custody thinking that they were operating under the laws of war only to find themselves later confronted by federal judges demanding that their intelligence serve as evidence. The mismatch has caused huge problems. Data good enough to inform a probabilistic intelligence assessment that a given detainee is worth holding are often useless as evidence before a judge used to hearing from live witnesses. Records of interviews with former detainees that might reasonably convince an intelligence analyst that another detainee had signed up with the enemy may not move a judge with no access to those witnesses, particularly amid allegations that the interviewees had faced maltreatment while in custody. In other words, while the current system produces too little review too late and too erratically to benefit the detainees, it produces an environment in which government officials have no idea what they can do today safe in the knowledge that the courts will stand by them down the road.

Indeed, even today, most of the central questions whose answers necessarily make up any detention system remain wide open. The Supreme Court, in deciding that the federal courts have jurisdiction over habeas corpus cases from Guantánamo, gave only the barest sketch of what the proceedings should look like, leaving a raft of questions open for district and appellate court judges:

—Who bears the burden of proof in these cases, and what is that burden—that is, who has to prove what?

—What are the boundaries of the president's detention power—that is, assuming that the government can prove that a detainee is who it claims him to be, what sort of person is it lawful to detain?

—What sort of evidence can the government use?

—How should the courts handle intelligence data or evidence that may have been given involuntarily?

None of those questions—or many others besides—has a solid answer on which either detainees or the government can rely. In a few discrete areas, judges have developed a relatively strong consensus. In others, they have disagreed profoundly. As Judge Thomas Hogan—who handled common issues for most of the judges on the district court in Washington—put it in a hearing in December 2009, "we have been operating under procedures drawn up by the court, and principally [by] myself, and the judges who have adopted much of these procedures [are operating] in a new venue that has been untested." The result is that "we have . . . in this court now a difference in substantive law that will be applied among the District Court judges. . . . We have different rules and procedures being used by the judges, [and] different rules of evidence being used by the judges."[1] Although the oversight of the D.C. Circuit Court of Appeals to date has imposed some uniformity on the district court in the months since Judge Hogan's remarks and that trend can be expected to continue, the stability of the D.C. Circuit's positions over time is not a sure thing. The D.C. Circuit is not, after all, the final word on the rules; its decisions may be merely steps on the way to the Supreme Court.

Indeed, so fundamentally have the district court judges disagreed—and about such basic questions—that their differences have almost certainly affected the outcomes of the individual cases that they have decided. That is, detainees freed by certain district court judges would likely have had the lawfulness of their detentions affirmed if other judges with different standards had heard their cases. And the converse also is true.

In other words, within the contours of a system that looks structurally quite different from what any sensible political system would design, the emerging law of detention remains sharply disputed. There are several possible answers to each of a bewildering array of questions, with individual district judges and combinations of appellate judges picking and choosing among many possible permutations. The judges' choices are very different from one another, and the efforts of the D.C. Circuit Court of Appeals to resolve the differences may or may not prove to have legs.

By the time this book is published, the landscape will have changed. New opinions will have come down. We will likely have greater clarity on certain points, and points on which we now feel relatively certain will have come into doubt. What almost certainly will not have changed, however, is the sense that the system is up for grabs, that it is being defined in use, and that it could turn dramatically in any of several directions in relatively short order. I offer the following account of the emerging law—obsolete though it may soon be—to illustrate the uncertainty that this sort of process generates.

Start with the most basic questions of all: who bears the burden of proof, and what is it? Does the government have to prove that the detainee is part of whatever class of people it may lock up, or does the detainee have to prove that he is not? To people conditioned by criminal law norms, the answer to these questions may seem obvious, and so far, the district court judges have unanimously held that the government should bear the burden of proving that a detainee satisfies the grounds for detention and that it must do so by the preponderance of the evidence. Some of those judges have done so with explicit reference to the criminal law. Judge Gladys Kessler, for example, wrote in one case that "[j]ust as a criminal defendant need not prove his innocence, a detainee need not prove that he was acting innocently. . . . [T]he fact that the Petitioner may not be able to offer neat answers to every factual question posed by the Government does not relieve the Government of its obligation to satisfy its burden of proof."[2]

That position, however, isn't obvious at all, and the D.C. Circuit has conspicuously declined to embrace it. The Supreme Court has not specified the nature of the burden of proof in these cases, but it did appear to assume in *Boumediene* that the government rather than the petitioner would bear that burden. On the other hand, in an earlier case, the justices suggested that the government might be entitled to a rebuttable presumption in favor of its evidence—which would seem to cut the other way. The D.C. Circuit is clearly interested in the question. After oral argument in the very case in which Judge Kessler wrote the words quoted above, the judges ordered a briefing on whether preponderance of the evidence is really the correct standard. Detainees' lawyers have consistently urged a higher burden on the government, while the court was clearly inviting the government to argue for a lower burden—a possibility that it had raised in an earlier opinion.

Because the government declined to argue for a lower standard, the judges ultimately wrote, "we are thus left with no adversary presentation on an important question affecting many pending cases in this court and in the district court" and thus "will not decide the question in this case." That said, the court expressed considerable "doubt . . . that the [Constitution] requires the use of the preponderance standard."[3] Even the most basic questions of all remain potentially in play.

Giving the burden of proof to the government has proven significant in several merits decisions, all of which involved detainees who failed to offer credible exculpatory accounts of their activities. In those cases, judges openly doubted the petitioners' credibility, describing their versions of the events in their respective cases as "implausible," "troubling," and "fantastic."[4] But because the burden of proof lies with the government, the judges observed, the petitioners' lack of credibility did not permit the government to prevail. They determined instead that even though it was unlikely that the events occurred as the petitioners contended, the government had not established the likelihood that its version was accurate either—and therefore they ruled in favor of the detainees. (An opinion handed down as this book went to press suggests that at least one district court judge may be reconsidering that approach.)

Even if we knew for sure which party bears the burden of proof and what it is, we would still have to ask the question of *what exactly that party has to prove.* The question of whom to detain is one of the subtlest and most important questions at issue in any detention system. There are any number of ways in which one can define the class of people subject to noncriminal detention, and current law offers only the most limited guidance as to the permissible bounds of that authority. Unsurprisingly, therefore, different judges propose substantially different standards. At least for now, the D.C. Circuit has taken a broad view of the government's detention power, but the question is certain to generate subsequent appeals.

The Bush administration took the position that it could detain for the duration of hostilities both members and supporters of entities—including al Qaeda, the Taliban, and "associated forces"—engaged in hostilities against the United States or its allies. The Obama administration narrowed that claim slightly, asserting that its detention authority extends to members and *substantial* supporters of enemy groups. That was something of a non-change, since the Bush administration had not detained anybody on grounds that the person had *insubstantially* supported the enemy. But the position of both administrations raised several questions with which the courts have struggled since: What does it mean to be "part of" enemy forces? Are supporters, substantial or not, inside or outside of the detainable class? Is it enough to be part of or to support the enemy or does one have to be dangerous too?

Several district court judges have accepted that the congressional authorization to use military force confers authority on the executive branch to detain those who are *part of* al Qaeda, the Taliban, and associated forces but rejected the proposition that independent *support*—even if substantial—provides a distinct ground for detention. The wrinkle here is that those judges acknowledged that "no settled criteria" exist for identifying formal membership in al Qaeda, so the courts must be open to proof of *functional* membership—as evidenced by, among other things, support. The key inquiry, one of the judges wrote, is "whether the individual functions or participates within or under the command structure of the organization—i.e., whether he receives and executes orders or directions."[5]

By contrast, one judge on the district court and, more important, the court of appeals accepted the possibility that detention may be justified not just for formal and functional members but also for a person who has provided support independently. The D.C. Circuit, in fact, construed the AUMF to justify not just the narrower support ground that the Obama administration favors, but also the original Bush administration variant, in which support did not necessarily have to qualify as substantial. In the D.C. Circuit's view, those who "purposely and materially support" enemy forces are subject to detention.[6]

At the other extreme, one judge took the view that the AUMF authorizes detention only when it is "necessary to prevent those individuals from rejoining the battle" and thus authorizes detention only when the detainee has a "current likelihood of rejoining the enemy" or poses a current threat.[7] The D.C. Circuit has since rejected that view, though detainees will surely raise it again in future appeals. In other words, judicial opinion on the definition of the detainable class ranges from a highly restrictive view in which the government may detain people only when it can make a specific showing that they would otherwise rejoin enemy forces to a broad view in which the government may lock up anyone who gave support to the enemy, even if the person gave it wholly independently.

To illustrate my earlier point about the interrelations between these detention cases and operations in theater, consider for a moment how the different messages that these two rules send would affect the Mark Martins problem if either rule were firmly established. That is, what message would they send to commanders in the field and to those offering them legal advice? Confronted with, say, a fortified compound populated by people who are known to support the enemy but who are not necessarily "part of" the enemy in any direct sense, one approach would seem to regard an attack as authorized by the AUMF; the more restrictive approach would appear to regard it as something of a question. The fact that no habeas judge would ever review the matter probably would not make these judicial opinions any less of a source of law bearing on such questions—a source of law that military lawyers would feel bound to study and try to apply.

A question closely related to the formal scope of the president's detention authority concerns whether a showing adequate to support a detention is, once established, etched in stone or whether time or intervening events can weaken it. That question shows up repeatedly in these cases, and judges have taken strikingly different positions on it. Put simply, is a finding of eligibility for detention immutable in the sense that having once been a member or supporter of a terrorist group, an individual can always be detained? Or can changed circumstances vitiate the underlying relationship, so that detention is no longer a legal option? And if a relationship can be vitiated, does the detainee bear the burden of proving that vitiation took place or does the government bear the burden of proving that a relationship still exists?

Two distinct issues lurk in this broad set of questions. The first is whether the passage of time in some fashion affects the government's evidentiary burden, so that evidence that would suffice to justify detention at an earlier stage no longer suffices at the point of habeas review. Does the same standard that the judges apply in habeas review theoretically apply at the point that the government acquires custody of a person or does the standard applied somehow change over the course of detention? In other words, does the government bear some escalating evidentiary burden as time goes on?

That question is not merely an academic one. Detention operations take place in the shadow of the body of substantive and procedural law that the judges are developing in these habeas proceedings, including the burden of proof that the government ultimately must meet. Even if it were clear that the preponderance standard applied only at the point of habeas review, personnel all along the chain of custody could be expected to factor that into their decisionmaking and evidence collection process, provided that some realistic prospect of eventual judicial review existed. If the signals emerging from the habeas proceedings indicate instead that the preponderance standard applies uniformly throughout the period of custody, this effect will be even stronger. One way or the other, therefore, those determining whether to take custody of an individual in the first instance or how to process him over time will take account of the rulings on this point. It will affect either commanders at temporary screening facilities who are determining whether to continue to hold an individual or long-term detention review tribunals operating in connection with theater internment facilities—or both.

None of the judges has addressed this issue directly; however, it is latent in many of their opinions. It remains submerged because the judges never seem to challenge the propriety of the initial decision to take a suspect into custody or later decisions by military screening officials to continue holding him. At the same time, they feel obligated in retrospect to examine the evidence supporting the detention with a degree of care that nobody would apply or demand in the field or in the screening process. Inherent in that approach is the understanding that, at some point after capture, the bar is raised.

All of the judges take this approach to some degree, though the degree seems to vary. At the deferential end of the spectrum, Judge James Robertson described the evidence in one case before him as "gossamer thin" and "of a kind fit only for these unique proceedings . . . and ha[ving] very little weight." However, he nonetheless ruled that the president had the authority to detain the petitioner because "[c]ombat operations in Afghanistan continue to this day and—in my view—the President's 'authority to detain for the duration of the relevant conflict' which is 'based on longstanding law-of-war principles' has yet to 'unravel.'" In other words, the evidence may be lousy, but if it ever justified the detention, it still does and it will for the duration of the current conflict.[8] (The D.C. Circuit, in affirming that opinion, later described the same evidence as "so strong," a disparity that reveals just how disputed the evaluation of evidence in these cases really is.[9])

Yet even in this case, the discussion of the evidence was detailed, probing, and skeptical, far more so than the review in any field tribunal or screening process conducted under the laws of war would be. What's more, the stated standard that the court purported to apply—placing on the government the burden of proof by a preponderance of the evidence—seems considerably more stringent than the test for an *initial* detention decision.

The other district judges have all seemed to go considerably further than Judge Robertson. While none ever questioned the initial decision to detain a suspect, they all seemed to suggest that evidence that may have justified the initial detention will not serve in retrospect to convince a court to bless it. These judges suggested that some degree of temporal shift had occurred in their assessment of evidence, though none of them clearly addressed precisely *how* the evidentiary standard had changed over the course of detention. Nor did they make clear at what point evidence initially suitable to detain a person became unsuitable or whether the government was obliged to meet an incrementally increasing standard the longer detention continued.

The second issue is whether a relationship adequate to support a detention, once established, can be severed, making a once-lawful detention no longer lawful. The judges have addressed this question directly. While they agree in a highly general way that to justify a detention the government must establish that some meaningful relationship links a detainee with an enemy organization, they do not agree even at that level of generality about the circumstances under which a person can withdraw from such a relationship.

In one case, Judge Ellen Segal Huvelle found that events occurring *subsequent to capture*—indeed, events occurring while the detainee spent time in U.S. custody—sufficed to vitiate an otherwise adequate relationship to al Qaeda and therefore required the detainee's release. In that instance, as summarized in the *Washington Post*, the petitioner had joined al Qaeda and learned how to use weapons at an al Qaeda training facility. "By late 2001 . . . [he] was hiding with bin Laden and others in the mountains of Tora Bora, where he acted as a cook and a fighter," the paper reported. Subsequently, Pakistani officials captured him and turned him over to U.S. authorities.[10] According to Judge Huvelle, while in Guantánamo the petitioner cooperated fully with the government, which resulted in beatings and threats to his life from other detainees. He stated that "[m]y family and I are threatened to be killed . . . and this threat happened here in prison . . . many times." His cooperation became public knowledge when "the *Washington Post* published a front-page article regarding [his] cooperation, specifically citing him by name." Given his cooperation and the public knowledge of it, Judge Huvelle concluded that he "can no longer constitute a threat to the United States" and ordered him released.[11] In other words, the fact that he became a cooperating witness against his fellows while in captivity—and the fact that his cooperation became known—served to vitiate a conceded prior relationship and therefore could unravel the legality of his detention.

Other judges explicitly disagreed with Judge Huvelle on the relevance of future dangerousness (and the court of appeals has now rejected her view), and they seemed to agree that the relevant question is whether the detainee was a member *at the time of capture*, not what happened later. They also appeared to agree on the possibility that a detainee can sever a relationship prior to capture, but they applied very different standards in deciding whether a relationship in fact continued to exist up until that point.

Sometimes, the question is easy enough. For example, in one case, Judge Richard Leon confronted a detainee who had briefly joined al Qaeda but whose relationship with the group quickly soured. The petitioner stayed for five days at an al Qaeda–affiliated guesthouse and eighteen days at an al Qaeda training camp. Judge Leon describes this relationship as "at best—in its formative stage." At the training camp, however, al Qaeda leaders suddenly suspected the petitioner of spying on them and then tortured him "for months into giving a false confession." The Taliban then imprisoned the petitioner "for a substantial eighteen-plus month period." Judge Leon regarded it as obvious that that sequence of events sufficed to vitiate whatever relationship had existed, and it is hard to disagree.[12]

On the other hand, another judge—Judge Kessler—found that a different detainee's relationship with al Qaeda had similarly terminated prior to his capture, despite a rather different fact pattern and much less compelling evidence of a break. Once again, the government relied on evidence that the petitioner had attended an al Qaeda training camp, and the petitioner claimed to have departed the training early under bad terms with the sponsors. Yet not only did he not claim to have been detained or abused as a result of that falling out, he claimed that he was spared such treatment on account of his sister's recent marriage to a man with close ties to Osama bin Laden. Indeed, this petitioner had become an al Qaeda trainee after having traveled to Kandahar with his sister "to attend a celebration of the marriage" hosted by bin Laden himself. The petitioner met bin Laden there and met with him again a few days later; he then went on to stay at a Taliban guesthouse and to attend the al Qaeda training camp.

Judge Kessler concluded that the detainee's initial relationship with al Qaeda seemed to have been primarily familial in nature and that his subsequent enrollment as an al Qaeda trainee had not resulted in a continuing relationship. It had lasted only seven to ten days, and no evidence suggested that he went on to occupy a structured role in the hierarchy of enemy forces. The petitioner's "conduct after training at Al Farouq does not demonstrate that . . . [he] took any affirmative steps to align himself with al-Qaida. . . . The Government offered no substantive evidence that he continued on a course of substantial support for al-Qaida." Judge Kessler thus determined both that the petitioner's relationship with al Qaeda never reached a level sufficient to detain him and that whatever relationship did exist had been vitiated.[13] The D.C. Circuit later reversed that opinion in disparaging terms, writing on the vitiation point that "there was no evidence that [he] ever affirmatively disassociated himself from al-Qaida, even though he 'accepted his expulsion.'"[14]

Judge James Robertson—the same judge who had found "gossamer thin" evidence sufficient in the case described above—even found for a detainee who acknowledged swearing an oath of loyalty to al Qaeda and presented *no* evidence of subsequent withdrawal. Indeed, in this case the judge found that the detainee had joined al Qaeda in the early 1990s and had maintained sporadic contact with high-level al Qaeda operatives in the years that followed. He had wired small amounts of money on behalf of a senior al Qaeda figure. He had known an al Qaeda operative in Canada who tried to bomb the Los Angeles International Airport. Some of the September 11 hijackers had even briefly stayed at his apartment. Yet while the detainee offered no evidence that he had ever left the group, the court ruled that the government had failed to show that he had enough engagement over the years that followed his oath to establish a vital ongoing relationship. The court held that, in effect, he had let his membership lapse.[15] The question of what a detainee has to show to establish that a relationship is no longer vital or what the government has to show to establish that it remains vital is still one of the most important questions outstanding before the habeas courts.

All of this ferment deals only with the *substantive* dimensions of detention—the questions of whom the government can detain pursuant to what sort of standards. In many ways, however, the most difficult questions are procedural and evidentiary: What kind of materials can the government use to prove its case, assuming that it's the government's case to prove?

In many, if not most, of the habeas cases, the government has depended heavily on various kinds of out-of-court hearsay statements. Some are contained in documents specifically generated for purposes of the habeas litigation, such as affidavits or declarations from military or government personnel. Often, however, the key statements appear in documents generated originally for other purposes. Those documents include intelligence reports that record or summarize information provided by various sources; records and summaries of statements made by detainees during interrogation; and transcripts and summaries of statements made by detainees when appearing before Combatant Status Review Tribunals (CSRTs) and Administrative Review Boards (ARBs)— the administrative panels that the Bush administration set up to review detentions. All of these types of documents present difficult questions in terms of their admissibility and probative value.

The judges do seem to agree on one central point: hearsay must be "reliable" in order to factor into the court's analysis of the merits of a habeas case. From there, however, things get complicated. As a threshold matter, the judges appear to disagree on whether reliability is a necessary condition for admissibility or simply a critical factor in assessing the weight to be given to the evidence. The D.C. Circuit seems to have resolved that question, at least for now, by ruling that hearsay is always admissible and that its reliability affects only the weight that the evidence will receive.[16] Setting that issue aside, the actual application of the reliability standard across numerous cases has generated a remarkably complex group of decisions. They seem to reflect both some underlying assumptions shared by the judges and a healthy dose of the judges' personal sense of fairness and level of comfort with material quite different from the sort of evidence that they normally see.

In short, while the judges appear to agree on "reliability" as the appropriate test for hearsay, they have very different opinions on what degree of vetting and corroboration is required to render hearsay reliable. As a result, judges use much the same vocabulary to describe rulings that differ significantly.

Then there's the matter of involuntary statements, whether hearsay or not. In a criminal proceeding, involuntary statements are simply inadmissible and custodial interrogation is regarded as so inherently coercive that the Supreme Court has generally required, as a prophylactic matter, that judges exclude statements obtained without prior warning of their potential legal consequences. Yet in these cases, all interrogations involve detainees held for long periods of time and questioned repeatedly without warnings or access to counsel. In many of them the government places great weight on detainee statements—either inculpatory admissions by detainees about themselves or statements about other detainees—and allegations of coercion have arisen frequently. To frame the question simply, when is an interrogation sufficiently coercive to require either exclusion of a resulting statement from evidence or a significant diminution of the weight that it is accorded?

As of this writing the D.C. Circuit has not addressed this issue, but the district court has done so repeatedly, and its judges have varied widely in their approaches to it. It is entirely unclear what substantive test the judges are employing in distinguishing between interrogation statements that can be admitted and credited and those that cannot. At this stage, we know only that the mere fact of being in long-term military custody without access to counsel does not alone suffice to make statements inadmissible and that certain especially brutal forms of interrogation will put detainee statements off limits.

At one end of the spectrum, Judge Robertson appeared quite dismissive in one case of a petitioner's claim that, as the judge put it, "any incriminating statements he made were made 'as a result of torture, the threat of torture or coercion and are therefore unreliable.'" He dealt with the claim only in a footnote (at least in the redacted version of the opinion) and spent very few words evaluating it beyond noting that only one allegation of coercion is "specific." That allegation, Judge Robertson noted, is "that interrogators threatened to withhold medical treatment until . . . [the petitioner] provided them information. The government retorts that interrogators' notes reveal that . . . [the petitioner] was provided care and that he used his medical condition as an excuse to avoid answering difficult questions." Judge Robertson did not address the issue further, a fact that presumably reflects his acceptance of the government's explanation and his willingness to give weight to these allegedly coerced statements. As a result, he had no occasion to address where the line might lie between interrogation methods that are and are not appropriate for generating evidence.[17]

In contrast to that apparently casual treatment, other judges express considerable concern about the issue of coercion. They refuse to give any weight to evidence that may have been gained by—or tainted by—coercive methods, and they seem far readier to credit claims of coercion. Yet they too generally fail to identify precisely where the line lies or what standard they are following. Some suggest that the relevant issue is "torture"; one suggests that it is failure to follow the Army Field Manual on interrogation; others suggest that it is whether statements were made voluntarily. Looking at the jurisprudence to date, the military would have little certainty as to what behavior today will yield admissible statements tomorrow.

Where Judge Robertson discounts allegations of coercion in the face of plausible government denials, Judge Kessler tacks in the other direction, discounting evidence that the government *may* have gained through the use or threat of coercive methods even in the absence of clear evidence of abuse. In her rulings, even a witness's *fear of potential mistreatment* suffices to call a statement into question. In one opinion, for example, she suggested that merely giving a statement at a site where abuse was taking place—even if the abuse involved someone *other* than the detainee—is grounds for doubting the value of that statement. Regarding evidence that a detainee had received military training, she wrote that the witness in question "made the inculpatory statement at Bagram Prison in Afghanistan, about which there have been widespread, credible reports of torture and detainee abuse." She concluded that "[a]ny effort to peer into the mind of a detainee at Bagram, who admitted to fearing torture at a facility known to engage in such abusive treatment, simply does not serve to rehabilitate a witness whose initial credibility must be regarded as doubtful." Regarding another piece of evidence, she stated that the witness's testimony "has been cast in significant question, due to the fact that it was elicited at Bagram amidst actual torture or fear of it."[18] Judge Kessler seems to treat the mere fact that coercion took place in the facility holding the detainee as presumptive grounds for discounting any statement by that detainee.

The judges also vary considerably on the question of taint. In the criminal context, a coerced statement can taint—and thus preclude the use of—a later statement that was not itself the direct product of coercion. If the police beat a confession out of a suspect and later ask him nicely to repeat that confession, the burden falls on the government to show that the second statement is not an indirect result of the beating. While the judges all appear to accept that brutal treatment can taint later statements in the habeas context too, they appear to differ sharply with respect to how to apply a taint analysis in practice.

To cite one example, Judge Hogan concluded that twenty-three statements given by one petitioner were "tainted by coercive interrogation techniques [and] therefore . . . lack . . . sufficient indicia of reliability." The government did not contest that the detainee in question had suffered brutal treatment before coming to Guantánamo and did not try to use the statements that he gave as a result of that treatment. Instead, it sought to rely on statements that he subsequently gave under less problematic conditions at Guantánamo. Judge Hogan ruled, however, that those statements were tainted by the prior abuse and thus could not be considered either. Yet he did ultimately admit some of the detainee's post-abuse statements—specifically, statements made in the context of three CSRT and ARB proceedings. He explained that in those settings the lingering taint of prior abuse was overcome by the formality of the setting and the additional protection that formality afforded. Unfortunately for the detainee, the evidence admitted from those hearings satisfied Judge Hogan that he was lawfully detained.[19]

Yet not all the judges regard the more formal setting of the review hearings as clearing the taint of prior abuse. Judge Ricardo Urbina, for example, confronted a case in which a detainee had confessed to attending al Qaeda's Al Farouq training camp and to staying at a guesthouse used by al Qaeda to facilitate the intake of its trainees. Those confessions took place both when the detainee was being interrogated and when he appeared before a CSRT. Yet in the later habeas proceedings, the detainee sought to recant his Al Farouq admission, arguing that he was tortured while in U.S. custody in Afghanistan, that he falsely confessed to attending Al Farouq during interrogation sessions only in order to avoid abuse, and that he repeated that confession before his CSRT because he believed "he would be punished if he gave the tribunal a different account than what he had previously told interrogators." The situation, in other words, closely resembled the one that Judge Hogan faced. In contrast to Judge Hogan, however, Judge Urbina did not carve out an exception for CSRT statements but treated them as equally tainted and thus unworthy of consideration.[20]

To put the matter simply, it is utterly unclear today what interrogation methods will or will not produce admissible statements and how long and under what circumstances the taint of coercive interrogations will persist. Given the reliance of U.S. forces on interrogation in day-to-day overseas operations as well as the frequency with which they take custody of people previously held and interrogated by other governments, that lack of clarity creates enormous uncertainty.

At a more overarching level, the judges have also taken rather different approaches to broad questions of how to read evidence. Specifically, the judges have struggled over whether to assess individual allegations made by the government as if they are akin to elements of a criminal offense or whether to take a more impressionistic view of the overall picture, using what the intelligence community calls the "mosaic theory" of evidence.

The mosaic theory has long described a relatively straightforward strategy for intelligence analysis under which items of information that are individually trivial become significant when aggregated with other such pieces of information. The mosaic formed by these "tiles" can be highly illuminating, even though it is made up of individually useless scraps. At one level, this form of analysis is no different from routine courtroom use of circumstantial evidence. Yet some of the judges have bristled at it—both insisting that the tiles be highly reliable and questioning whether it is even proper to amalgamate seemingly innocuous data to mine its latent probative value.

In identical language in several cases, for example, Judge Kessler noted that it "may well be true" that the mosaic "approach is a common and well-established mode of analysis in the intelligence community." Nonetheless, "at this point in this long, drawn-out litigation the Court's obligation is to make findings of fact and conclusions of law which satisfy appropriate and relevant legal standards as to whether the Government has proven by a preponderance of the evidence that the Petitioner is justifiably detained." She added that the "kind and amount of evidence which satisfies the intelligence community in reaching final conclusions about the value of information it obtains may be very different, and certainly cannot govern the Court's ruling."[21]

In a subsequent case, she appeared to challenge the very notion that the government might prevail based on circumstantial evidence. In response to government pleas, as she puts it, "not to examine in isolation individual pieces of evidence . . . but rather to evaluate them 'based on the evidence as a whole,'" she dismissed this "mosaic approach," arguing that the evidence must "be carefully analyzed—major-issue-in-dispute by major-issue-in-dispute—since the whole cannot stand if its supporting components cannot survive scrutiny." In practice, Judge Kessler's approach makes it extraordinarily difficult for the government to prevail. She proceeded in this case to describe the government's having proven "by far more than a preponderance of the evidence" that the petitioner had "traveled extensively in Europe, both before and after September 11, 2001, by using false names, passports, and other official documents"; that "while in London Petitioner attended mosques that were well known to have radical, fundamentalist clerics advocating jihad"; that at one of those mosques he "met a recruiter who then paid for and arranged his trip to Afghanistan along routes well-traveled by those wishing to fight with al-Qaida and/or the Taliban"; and that "he stayed at a guesthouse with direct ties to al-Qaida and its training camps." She even found specifically that he had the intent to join the enemy.

All that, however, proved not to be good enough, because the government had not proven that he had taken training or fought. Without that additional item of proof that he had actually submitted to the command structure of an enemy organization, Judge Kessler was unwilling to draw overall inferences about the likelihood of his membership from the lesser, probative facts that she found: "In short, at the point in his journey where the

Government's evidence fails, Petitioner had not yet acquired a role within the 'military command structure' of al-Qaida and/ or the Taliban, nor acquired any membership in these enemy forces. One who merely follows a path, however well-trodden, from London to Afghanistan and ends up staying in an al-Qaida-affiliated guesthouse, cannot be said to occupy a 'structured' role in the 'hierarchy' of the enemy force."[22]

By contrast, other judges take a far more impressionis-tic approach, looking at the overall picture that the pattern of evidence creates. The D.C. Circuit appears strongly inclined in that direction. In July 2010, the court of appeals handed down a major rebuke to Judge Kessler on precisely this point, in the case described above of the Yemeni man, Mohammed Al-Adahi, who went to Afghanistan, had his sister's wedding hosted by bin Laden, met with bin Laden individually, and then trained at Al Farouq. In contrast to Kessler, the circuit panel treated the mosaic question as a matter of what it termed "conditional probability analysis," the likelihood of a particular fact's being true given the truth of a different fact:

> Those who do not take into account conditional probability are prone to making mistakes in judging evidence. They may think that if a particular fact does not itself prove the ultimate proposition (e.g., whether the detainee was part of al-Qaida), the fact may be tossed aside and the next fact may be evaluated as if the first did not exist. . . . This is precisely how the district court proceeded in this case: Al-Adahi's ties to bin Laden "cannot prove" he was part of Al-Qaida and this evidence therefore "must not distract the Court." . . . The fact that Al-Adahi stayed in an al-Qaida guesthouse "is not in itself sufficient to justify detention." . . . Al-Adahi's attendance at an al-Qaida training camp "is not sufficient to carry the Government's burden of showing that he was a part" of al-Qaida. . . . And so on. The government is

right: the district court wrongly "required each piece of the
government's evidence to bear weight without regard to all
(or indeed any) other evidence in the case. This was a fundamental mistake that infected the court's entire analysis."

The result is that whereas Judge Kessler found the evidence
inadequate, the court of appeals found that it supported Al-Adahi's detention overwhelmingly.[23] Judge Kessler's opinion in this
case was something of an outlier, but the tendency to disaggregate
evidence rather than to view it as an impressionistic whole is common among some of the district judges. The difference between
this approach and the approach of the court of appeals in this
case is probably key to other pending appeals. Which one catches
on will ultimately determine the fate of a number of Guantánamo
detainees. More broadly, it will condition the type of evidentiary
fact patterns that government agencies will regard as adequate to
support a detention. Will they look probabilistically at an overall
portrait or will they look instead at whether they can prove individual key facts?

With the exception of the Al-Adahi case, it is impossible to
say with certainty that any given case would have come out differently if it had been heard by a judge other than the one who
heard it. Still, the approaches of the district and appellate court
judges to the Guantánamo habeas cases to date differ so markedly
on matters so fundamental that some are at least in grave tension
with others on the bottom-line question of whether to tolerate or
forbid continued detention given similar sets of facts.

There are at least three distinct categories of cases in which
differences of opinion among the judges arguably impact their
bottom-line holdings. First, there are cases involving the supposed
vitiation of a relationship cognizable under the laws of war or
the AUMF. Most notably, Judge Huvelle required a showing not
merely of a relationship at the time of capture but of *future* dangerousness—a position that several other judges and the D.C.

Circuit now explicitly reject. Judge Robertson, for example, expressly disclaimed any likelihood of future dangerousness in the case of a detainee who had lost a leg, writing at one point that "it seems ludicrous to believe that he poses a security threat now."²⁴ And the D.C. Circuit later ruled "that the United States's authority to detain an enemy combatant is not dependent on whether an individual would pose a threat to the United States or its allies if released but rather upon the continuation of hostilities."²⁵ At a minimum, the other judges appear likely to have decided quite differently from Judge Huvelle the case of a conceded operative who had become a cooperating witness while in captivity—and she too might have if her case had followed, rather than preceded, the D.C. Circuit's pronouncement.

The flip side of this point is that Judge Huvelle's approach to vitiation would, if it eventually catches on in later appeals, compel a different outcome in nearly all the cases in which other judges have refused to issue the writ. Judge Huvelle contended that "this Court must conclude that [the detainee's] current likelihood of rejoining the enemy is relevant to whether his continued detention is authorized under the law." And she described the government as bearing the "burden of establishing that . . . continued detention is authorized under the AUMF's directive that such force be used 'in order to prevent future acts of international terrorism.'"²⁶ Among the cases in which the judges sided with the government, none of the decisions could survive this future dangerousness inquiry. In no case did the government present evidence (at least not that the other judges discussed) of a detainee's likelihood of posing a threat, nor did it attempt to describe his likelihood of rejoining the fight. In many Guantánamo cases, there simply is not material in the record that would support a specific finding of future dangerousness.

Second are cases involving supposedly involuntary statements. It seems likely that the difference between Judge Hogan and Judge Urbina regarding allegedly involuntary statements and their tainting of later statements before review panels would have yielded different outcomes in both cases if either judge had heard the other's. Judge Hogan determined in his case that a detainee's prior coercion did not taint his statements in his CSRT and ARB hearings, where, according to the judge, the added protections of a more formal environment served to alleviate the detainee's fears of renewed maltreatment. The detainee's statements in those settings provided the entirety of the case against him. Yet Judge Urbina, faced with a similar problem in a different case, made no distinction between statements in the CSRT and statements to interrogators. Had Judge Hogan held similarly, he could not have denied the writ in the case that he decided.

By contrast, while Judge Urbina made clear that the CSRT statements that he excluded would not have swayed him had he admitted them, the same statements may well have satisfied Judge Hogan had he been hearing that case. They included admissions that the petitioner took training at Al Farouq and that he spent time riding in a car that shuttled food to the Taliban lines and was, as Judge Urbina put it, "surrounded by enemy armed forces."[27] That combination of training and association is quite similar to the facts that led Judge Hogan to consider the detainee in his case detainable, and it is almost as hard to imagine him failing to reach the same conclusion in Judge Urbina's case as it is to imagine Judge Urbina's affirming the detention in Judge Hogan's case.

Third and most speculative are cases involving the quantity of evidence needed for the government to meet its burden of proof. In some such cases one judge has affirmed a detention based on evidence that seems weaker than that on which another judge based his or her rejection of a detention. Consider the following cases.

In the first, Judge Robertson describes the proven facts, which he acknowledges to be "gossamer thin," as follows:

Up to this point, we have (a) a reasonable inference that Awad went to Kandahar to fight, (b) no reliable evidence that he was actually trained there, (c) undisputed evidence that he was in Mirwais Hospital during part of the siege, and (d) inconsistent evidence about how and when he arrived there. . . . The correlation among the names on the al Joudi list, the Tarnak Farms list, [TEXT REDACTED BY THE COURT] is too great to be mere coincidence. The [TEXT REDACTED BY THE COURT] I believe, . . . tip the scale finally in the government's favor.[28]

On that record, he affirmed the detention. The D.C. Circuit's later summary of the evidence makes it seem far more favorable to the government, but Judge Robertson treated the case as an extremely close one that hung by the thinnest of threads. In his account, at least, the case did not seem notably stronger than the one in which Judge Colleen Kollar-Kotelly, in granting the writ in one of her cases, described the proven facts as follows:

In summary, the Court has credited the Government's evidence that (1) Al Mutairi's path of travel into Afghanistan was consistent with the route used by al Wafa to smuggle individuals into Afghanistan to engage in jihad; (2) that Al Mutairi's travel from Kabul to a village near Khowst was consistent (in time and place) with the route of Taliban and al Qaida fighters fleeing toward the Tora Bora mountains along the Afghanistan-Pakistan border, and (3) Al Mutairi's non-possession of his passport is consistent with an individual who has undergone al Qaida's standard operating procedures that require trainees to surrender their passports prior to beginning their training. The Court has also found minimally probative on this record the appearance of Al Mutairi's name and reference to his passport [TEXT REDACTED IN ORIGINAL].

She also found that "Al Mutairi's described peregrinations within Afghanistan lack credibility." Yet faced with a detainee whose conduct was "consistent" with that of an al Qaeda recruit and whose own account was incredible, she issued the writ. She found that "[t]aking this evidence as a whole, the Government has at best shown that some of Al Mutairi's conduct is consistent with persons who may have become a part of al Wafa or al Qaida, but there is nothing in the record beyond speculation that Al Mutairi did, in fact, train or otherwise become a part of one or more of those organizations, where he would have done so, and with which organization." Because "the Government has not filled in these blanks nor supplanted Al Mutairi's version of his travels and activities with sufficiently credible and reliable evidence to meet its burden by a preponderance of the evidence," she ruled, he was entitled to the writ.[29] Would she have held the same had she known that the D.C. Circuit would later describe the evidence that Judge Robertson considered as "so strong"?

More strikingly, in the Al-Adahi case—the one described above that the D.C. Circuit Court reversed—Judge Kessler ruled for the detainee after describing the evidence as follows:

> When all is said and done, this is the evidence we have in this case. Al-Adahi probably had several relatives who served as bodyguards for Usama Bin Laden and were deeply involved with and supportive of al-Qaida and its activities. One of those relatives became his brother-in-law by virtue of marriage to his sister, [TEXT REDACTED BY THE COURT] Al-Adahi accompanied his sister to Afghanistan so that she could be with her husband and [TEXT REDACTED BY THE COURT]. The wedding celebration was held in Bin Laden's compound and many of his associates attended. At that celebration, Petitioner was introduced to Bin Laden, with whom he had a very brief conversation. Several days

later, the Petitioner had a five-to-ten-minute conversation with Bin Laden.

Thereafter, Petitioner stayed at an al-Qaida guesthouse for one night and attended the Al Farouq training camp for seven to ten days. He was expelled from Al Farouq for failure to obey the rules. . . . After his expulsion, Al-Adahi returned to the home of his sister and brother-in-law for several weeks and then traveled to other places in Afghanistan because he had no other obligations. Like many thousands of people, he sought to flee Afghanistan when it was bombed shortly after September 11, 2001.[30]

And she also found for the petitioner in a separate case, also described above, after describing the facts in the following manner:

Here, the Government has clearly proven, by far more than a preponderance of the evidence, that Petitioner traveled extensively in Europe, both before and after September 11, 2001, by using false names, passports, and other official documents. It has also proven, by far more than a preponderance of the evidence, that while in London Petitioner attended mosques which were well known to have radical, fundamentalist clerics advocating jihad. At one of the mosques he met a recruiter who then paid for and arranged his trip to Afghanistan along routes well-traveled by those wishing to fight with al-Qaida and/or the Taliban against the United States and its allies. Finally, the Government has also proved, by far more than a preponderance of the evidence, that once Petitioner arrived in Afghanistan he stayed at a guesthouse with direct ties to al-Qaida and its training camps.[31]

The records in these cases seem at least as compelling as the one on which Judge Robertson denied habeas. One has to imagine that neither Judge Kessler nor Judge Kollar-Kotelly would have denied the writ in the case in which Judge Robertson did. Furthermore, judging from the D.C. Circuit's opinions to date—its unreserved affirmance of Judge Robertson's judgment and its blistering reversal of Judge Kessler's—it also is hard to imagine that at least several of the judges on that court would agree with the standards and quantity of evidence that several of the district court judges are demanding. The D.C. Circuit has more than once stated that staying at an al Qaeda guesthouse or training at one of its facilities would *alone* offer "overwhelming" support to a detention judgment.[32]

Judge Robertson himself seems quite conflicted on the quantity of evidence question. For me, at least, it is hard to reconcile his upholding the detention discussed above on a concededly "gossamer thin" record with his decision a few months later to free the man who admitted that he had once sworn loyalty to Osama bin Laden and had maintained contacts with high-level terrorists since—and also provided occasional support to them. In that case, Judge Robertson summarized his findings as follows:

> The government had to adduce evidence—which is different from intelligence—showing that it was more *likely* than not that Salahi was "part of" al-Qaida. To do so, it had to show that the support Salahi undoubtedly did provide from time to time was provided within al-Qaida's command structure. The government has not done so. The government has shown that Salahi was an al-Qaida sympathizer—perhaps a "fellow traveler"; that he was in touch with al-Qaida members; and that from time to time, before his capture, he provided sporadic support to members of al-Qaida. . . .
>
> [T]he government wants to hold Salahi indefinitely, because of its concern that he might renew his oath to al-Qaida and become a terrorist upon his release. That concern

may indeed be well-founded. Salahi fought with al-Qaida in Afghanistan (twenty years ago), associated with at least a half-dozen known al-Qaida members and terrorists, and somehow found and lived among or with al-Qaida cell members in Montreal.[33]

The record in this case seems rather more than gossamer thin—though admittedly richer in innuendo than in hard facts. It is a classic case in which a judge more inclined toward a mosaic theory of the evidence—one based on the conditional probability analysis that the D.C. Circuit has since demanded—might come to a very different result. Yet Judge Robertson here granted the writ.

I do not mean to criticize any of the judges involved in these cases. To the contrary. The Supreme Court gave them a blank slate on which to write, with no guidance as to what they should be writing and with untold numbers of issues that they have to decide before they can deliver a bottom-line result. Nobody has stepped in to fill the void, and the result is that they have no choice but to make things up as they go along. In that context, judges have nowhere to look other than to their own instincts about fairness and about what facts they need to know in order to resolve matters confidently. It would be utterly surprising if their instincts were generally congruent with one another. These issues are, after all, rather hard, and they will divide judges no less than they divide other citizens.

The broad point, however, is that a policy of obfuscation does not obviate the need to design a coherent system of rules. It merely delegates the task to actors less visible and less accountable and in many respects more constrained than our political leadership. That might be defensible were the results of the delegation a set of policies with which we should rest easy. Then one might simply describe it as part of the balance that democracy strikes with expertise—much as we routinely delegate technically difficult policy questions to independent federal agencies or interest rate matters to the Federal Reserve Board.

But it's hard to look at any of the policy migrations that have taken place with respect to detention policy with anything like intellectual or emotional satisfaction. Should we really sleep better at night knowing that thousands of people whom U.S. forces either would have held or did in fact hold not too long ago now face detention instead at the hands of the Iraqi, Afghan, and Pakistani governments? Do we really feel better about Guantánamo detentions knowing that the rules are being thrashed out by judges in a haphazard fashion that, more than two years after *Boumediene*, has not really generated a coherent system of rules? Indeed, precisely because the judges have to focus on the specific cases in front of them, they do not focus principally on designing a system. That is instead a byproduct of their project—and it is not surprising that it's getting short shrift.

Whom exactly does this haphazard common-law development of a detention system serve? Surely not Mark Martins or the soldiers in the field who have to make decisions about whether to detain individuals and have today no idea of the substantive or evidentiary standards that they have to meet. Indeed, they don't even know with any confidence which detainees will end up before federal judges and which they can hold pursuant to their own administrative rules. It does not serve them.

One might argue that it serves detainees, on the theory that a zero-sum game of sorts exists between civil liberties and government power and that discomfiting detention authority therefore necessarily translates into greater freedom for detainees. But it doesn't. It translates into freedom for a few, proxy detention for a great many, and—let's face it—Predator drones for others. And it translates into random, unpredictable outcomes for the dwindling Guantánamo population.

What's more, it makes the broader political system look stupid. The obfuscation doesn't really work, after all. Nobody is fooled that the United States has really returned to a pre–September 11 paradigm, that we're out of the detention business, or that we have done much more than cover ourselves with a fig leaf—and a rather small fig leaf at that. Moreover, it's a fig leaf for which we pay a great price, the price of a detention system that actually suits our real needs. That has not emerged from the habeas litigation, and it almost certainly will not.

4

The Problems That
Denial Cannot Solve

Building a detention policy on a premise of obfuscation and denial is a project beset with problems. It both begins with and flatters a myth: that the United States does not do preventive detention. By flattering that myth, it both constrains and delegitimizes policymaking that greater candor would to some degree liberate. Because the nature of the project precludes any direct discussion of the contours of a reasonable detention system, it effectively delegates policymaking to bodies that should not be making U.S. military and national security policy—from corrupt and imperfect foreign proxy governments to domestic courts. Where rules emerge anyway, they do so slowly and fitfully and with little assurance that they will be well-tailored to contemporary needs. In short, our collective refusal to address directly the subject of detention produces long tarries on the road to bad policy.

It also inevitably produces incomplete policy. A society, after all, that assiduously strives to avoid the big questions concerning a difficult subject will inevitably succeed in avoiding at least a few of them. Each of those successes leaves a gap. These gaps tend to involve cases in which a crisis requires fast decision and action—the cases in which we simply don't have time to delegate. With respect to those questions, we either make the rules ourselves or we live with the uncertainty of not having any and fall back on whatever ill-fitting legal architecture makes itself available.

In this discussion, I focus on two such questions, both of which have already arisen repeatedly in the U.S. counterterrorism experience and both of which will almost certainly arise again. The first involves the acute emergency detention of a highly dangerous person (or group of persons) when the information available is imperfect and the stakes are high enough to put a premium on the detainee's short-term interrogation value. The second involves a situation in which U.S. forces once again capture large numbers of enemy forces—or enemy suspects—and have no reliable proxy on whom to offload them.

The first of these situations requires no particular imagination to foresee. It arises frequently, both in high-profile iterations and in relatively invisible ones. There are, for starters, incidents like the Christmas 2009 bombing attempt by Umar Farouk Abdulmutallab, who smuggled explosives in his underwear aboard a transatlantic flight bound for Detroit and tried to detonate them during landing, and the 2010 attempt by Faisal Shahzad to detonate a car bomb in Times Square. In such cases, authorities initially may or may not know whom they have captured; however, they urgently need to know what he knows. They also need to know how to categorize him: whether they should treat him as a criminal suspect or hold him as an enemy combatant under the laws of war and perhaps try him by a military commission. The answers to those questions might be heavily fact-dependent. Because the suspect is already in the United States, authorities cannot simply pawn him off on someone else. They have to make the decision themselves, and they do not have much time. There may, after all, be other would-be bombers in other planes in the air. Even if there are no other bombers, the people who sent the particular suspect will certainly vaporize if given enough time, and they will try to launch other attacks later. The absence of a clear system for handling such situations puts authorities in the position of having to guess what approach will best facilitate both short- and long-term intelligence collection and best guarantee long-term incapacitation and the retributive interests of the justice system.

Such situations have arisen episodically throughout the war on terror—even before September 11—and they tend to involve high-profile, relatively spectacular cases of near-miss terrorist attacks. The names of the various perpetrators—or would-be perpetrators—are well known: Richard Reid, Zacarias Moussaoui, Jose Padilla, and Ali Saleh Al-Marri, for example. And in each case, authorities have fallen back—with varying degrees of success—on the law available to them. In Reid's and Moussaoui's cases, they used criminal prosecution, and in Moussaoui's case they initially used the immigration detention system. In Padilla's and Al-Marri's cases, they used criminal process, then enemy combatant detention, then criminal process again. In the end, all of the men remained incarcerated for the duration, meaning that someone inclined to do so could see any of the cases as a success story of sorts. In all of these cases, the government satisfied at least its interest in incapacitating the individuals involved.

Yet in each case, the United States may also have paid a significant price for not having a system that better balances its incapacitation, intelligence gathering, and retributive needs. In some of the cases, like those of Reid and Moussaoui, serving the country's incapacitation and criminal justice interests meant that authorities never got the chance to conduct a sustained, serious interrogation of a suspect who presumably had important time-sensitive information about al Qaeda. In other cases, those involving Padilla and Al-Marri, for example, satisfying short-term interrogation interests ultimately compromised the government's long-term criminal case; as a result, both men ended up with embarrassingly light sentences that will free them from prison while they are still young enough to do great harm.

Another iteration of the same problem, which has arisen less visibly but still with some frequency, involves overseas captures, in, say, safe-house raids in Pakistan. They may net authorities one very big fish and a bunch of unidentified smaller fish. These days, U.S. forces seem to be leaving all such fish in the hands of Pakistani forces, but that has not always been possible—and the viability of this option depends to a great degree on the rather volatile health of cooperation between the United States and Pakistan on security matters at any given time. Such situations are complicated because authorities may have no idea whom they have captured—only that he was residing in close quarters with a big-time terrorist. But for precisely that reason, they have both an abiding intelligence interest and an abiding incapacitation interest in this sort of person. After all, some rather large percentage of people living or staying in a safe house with a major terrorist will turn out, on closer inspection, to be at least minor terrorist figures in their own right, and authorities can reasonably expect them to know quite a lot about the network that surrounds the captured leader.

But that will not always be the case. In one of the Guantánamo cases, a court found that a young man captured in a Pakistani raid on a Faisalabad safe house connected with Abu Zubaydah was in fact a student unconnected to al Qaeda who had come over for dinner with a friend, stayed the night, and been caught up in the raid.[1] Precisely because authorities may have little idea whom they have on their hands, they may have no immediate criminal justice option in these situations, since residence and association alone presumably violate no criminal laws. Again, the clock ticks quickly. If U.S. forces do not take custody of the suspects, they may lose the chance. If they have no noncriminal detention option, in other words, they may have no authority to assume custody at all.

A closely related variant of this problem arises when a foreign government captures a suspect—often using intelligence provided by the United States—but then either has no basis under its own law to hold him or lacks the political will do so. The choice facing the United States in such cases can be stark: take the suspect or watch him go free. Once again, intelligence that may provide a compelling basis to disrupt a group or individual may come nowhere near the standard necessary to convict a suspect in federal court. So in the absence of some authority extrinsic to the criminal justice system to hold such a person, for a short time or a long time, the government may lack the authority even to take custody of him.

In the past, the United States has tended to fall back on enemy combatant detention in all such situations. Various Guantánamo detainees fell into U.S hands in scenarios much like the ones described here. Some, like various people taken in safe-house raids, are still at Guantánamo. Others, like the Bosnian Algerian detainees turned over to the United States after Bosnian authorities concluded that they had no basis to prosecute them, have become a human rights cause célèbre and have—with one exception—gone free. More recently, as I have discussed, the United States has turned the tables on its regional allies. Detainees who once were too hot for our allies to handle but whom we eagerly took on are now too hot for *us* to handle—and we leave them safely in foreign hands.

Yet nobody knows how long this admittedly convenient arrangement will last in Afghanistan, Pakistan, and Iraq. In any event, it is not available elsewhere. A great many countries around the world will assist the United States in taking down a terrorist cell within their territory if the CIA provides the information and logistical support needed to do so. But often they will not participate in the second or third acts of this drama: the short-term interrogation or the long-term incapacitation that needs to follow. That was the problem that gave rise to the rendition program in the 1990s, in which the CIA facilitated the transport of terror suspects from countries where they could be captured to countries that had outstanding orders for their arrest. After September 11, 2001, driven largely by the desire to take control of interrogations, the United States began taking and maintaining custody of the suspects itself. In short, the second act has shifted in various directions over the years. The critical point is that the United States cannot refuse as a programmatic matter to *have* a second act if it wants help in these cases in the first place. If it tries, either it will find itself holding in some indeterminate and uncertain legal status the detritus of the war on terror or it will have to rely on opportunistic renditions at some point in the detention process—assuming, of course, that it can find some country to which to send the suspect in question. Or, in the alternative, it will at some point set him free.

The acute detention scenario will vary as greatly as the circumstances produced by the combination of the imagination of terrorists and the acuity and luck of intelligence, military, and law enforcement authorities. What binds the variants together, however, are several basic features: time pressure, high political and security stakes, imperfect information requiring further intelligence, and the absence of an obvious proxy to do whatever U.S. forces cannot do. The last point could mean that we have no foreign proxy available to do a long-term detention when, for one reason or another, we cannot use our criminal justice apparatus. Or it could mean that we have no proxy available to conduct interrogations that our forces cannot or will not conduct. In such situations, there is simply no way to delegate the decisionmaking. U.S. forces cannot avoid handling these situations themselves, and the absence of a considered process for doing so only guarantees that we will use one or another ill-considered process. It guarantees a wrenching political battle over the highest-stakes cases. And perhaps most important, it guarantees that there will be no political or legal safe harbor if things go wrong, as they undoubtedly sometimes will. Whatever government is then in power will not be able to plaintively claim, hoping to placate the political opposition or an angry public, that it followed the regular order, for there will be no regular order—no presumptive way or ways to behave when confronting the hardest of cases. A policy of denial, in other words, will ensure that we decide how we want authorities to behave only in assigning recriminations for what, in retrospect, did not work.

Consider the case of Abdulmutallab. If any terrorist scenario should not have caught the U.S. legal or political system unprepared, that was it. After all, almost precisely the same thing had happened before, when Richard Reid tried to take down a transatlantic flight with a crude carry-on bomb. Given al Qaeda's interest in air travel and how close Reid came to success, something like Abdulmutallab's attempt could easily have been anticipated. In fact, it *was* anticipated. Keeping explosives and weapons off planes is precisely the reason that we screen people getting on them. Much of the tightening of airport security screening in the years since September 11 has tracked ever-more-sophisticated efforts to smuggle explosives past screeners. No more wearing shoes through the metal detectors? That's because of shoe-bomber Reid. No liquids? That's because of the plot in Britain to use liquid explosives to bring down multiple planes back in 2005. Abdulmutallab's plot was almost the prototype of the sort of attack that we expected.

And, to be sure, we had a legal system of sorts to handle his capture and interrogation, following the intelligence failures that allowed him on the plane in the first place. In important ways, it actually performed rather well. Authorities pulled Abdulmutallab off the plane, interrogated him briefly, read him his *Miranda* rights, and charged him with a crime. Before clamming up, he talked for a little while, giving apparently important information. And in the longer term, authorities persuaded him to cooperate more fully. All of that happened without compromising the eventual criminal case against him. The system, in other words, threaded a needle that it had failed to thread in several of the earlier cases, achieving a kind of rough balance between short-term interrogation needs, long-term interrogation needs, the need to incapacitate the enemy, and the demands of justice. It may have served none of those interests perfectly, but it appears to have served them all at least to some considerable degree. Whether that success flowed from luck or from good institutional performance or, as I suspect, some combination of the two, it was a success—probably the best outcome that we could have hoped for.

Yet even in success, the administration's approach nonetheless sparked a major political controversy. President Obama found himself battered by the political opposition for falling back on the criminal justice system—just as President Bush had found himself battered by the political opposition for *not* falling back on the criminal justice system but on the military detention apparatus instead. Obama found himself criticized for allowing Abdulmutallab to be read his rights and given counsel, just as his predecessor found himself criticized for *not* giving Jose Padilla and Yasser Esam Hamdi access to counsel. Thoughtful legal observers from across the political spectrum openly wondered whether defaulting to the criminal justice system jeopardized important interests and whether some period of noncriminal detention and interrogation would better serve the intelligence interests that seemed paramount at the moment of crisis. President Obama found himself facing a mirror image of the damnation faced by President Bush—all seemingly without any recognition by the political system that it was conducting a kind of pincer action against the presidency.

The problem, quite simply, is that none of the systems on which we sometimes fall back was designed with this problem in mind—not the criminal justice system; not the military detention system; not the material witness detention system, in which authorities held Padilla prior to his designation as an enemy combatant; and not the immigration detention system, in which authorities held Moussaoui in the days before the September 11 attacks. None embodies what the government really needs in such situations, which is a brief grace period in which to hold someone, interrogate him, and figure out whom it is dealing with *before making any big decisions*. And none reflects any kind of political consensus concerning how we should handle the acute crisis detention scenario. These systems reflect, rather, other political consensuses: how to hold and punish criminals, how to detain the enemy during wartime, and how to deport illegal migrants. They can, of course, be jury-rigged for service in crisis detentions, but the public can see the poor fit, and it rightly discomforts people. So when we stick Al-Marri or Padilla in a brig for years without any process, the political system notices that they are deprived of the rights promised by the criminal justice system. And when we grant those rights to Abdulmutallab in the moment of crisis itself, the polity wonders what would have happened if he had taken seriously the system's guarantee of his right to remain silent and if other bombers had happened to be in the air on other flights at the time. Neither question is unreasonable.

To be sure, sometimes it all works out rather well. The criminal justice system, under some circumstances, can operate as an excellent intelligence gathering tool. The United States has had a string of big successes within that system of late—Abdulmutallab is one; Najibullah Zazi is another; the would-be Times Square car bomber, Faisal Shahzad, is a third. In all of those cases, the justice system pushed potentially major terrorist figures relatively swiftly into a cooperative posture. Those successes suggest that conservatives have sometimes underestimated the capacity and utility of the criminal justice apparatus as an instrument for disrupting terrorism. It does not, however, indicate that that apparatus is the ideal instrument or that it has been optimally tuned to handle *all* crisis detentions. Indeed, there have been times when falling back on the criminal justice system has failed us—and it will happen again. There will come a time when there really are other planes in the air and the captive takes his *Miranda* rights seriously or when we simply lack the authority to take custody of someone whom it would be imprudent to free. There will come a time when we will miss having a crisis detention authority designed for the purpose at hand.

The second problem that a policy of denial and delegation cannot address involves situations in which U.S. forces once again have to detain large numbers of detainees. Realistically, delegating detention to regional proxies works only as long as two favorable conditions persist: a cooperative and reasonably capable proxy is available, and the number of detainees remains manageable. Right now, proxy detention looks attractive because the raw number of detainees has been declining over the very period of years during which we have bulked up the capacity of our proxies to manage detentions. The result is that we can turn a large number of detainees over to our allies—and promise to turn over more; we can release a bunch of others; we can resettle a smattering. And through that combination of actions we can maintain the fiction that we are getting out of the detention business.

But it requires no special stretch of the imagination to believe that the number of new detainees may suddenly once again begin approaching, or even exceeding, the number of detainees exiting U.S. custody. What's more, that may happen in a part of the world in which we initially have no reliable proxy to act as a buffer between our forces and our detainees. Precisely that scenario has played out twice in the last decade, once in Afghanistan and once in Iraq. One should not assume the inevitable availability of the now-significant detention capacity of those proxies. Today, after years of U.S. involvement and investment, the Afghan and Iraqi governments find themselves capable of taking responsibility for a wide swath of detention operations. Yet that capacity did not exist at the beginning of our conflicts in their countries. It is a created condition, not a found condition, and it took a long time to create. Between the time that the United States needed to detain tens of thousands of people and the time that it could create that condition, it had to do the detentions itself.

We can, I believe, expect something similar the next time that the United States has to engage the enemy in some other location. If one imagines the eventual necessity of significant U.S. military operations in, say, Somalia or Yemen and imagines further that those actions might yield a new influx of detainees, precisely the same failures of governance that require such operations would also prevent local governments from taking responsibility for detentions, at least for a while. Indeed, even now, the inability of Yemen's government to take responsibility for its detainees at Guantánamo is one of the principal constraints on the Obama administration's plans to close the facility. In the interim between the outset of the next conflict and the creation of some significant proxy capacity, U.S. forces will have to do their own—and, of course, Europe's—detention work once again.

We can, of course, indulge the fantasy that that will never happen. We have learned the lessons of the Bush administration, we can tell ourselves, and we know now that using detention invites a world of pain—from both a legal and a public diplomacy vantage point. Consequently, we have ramped up our ability to handle detentions through the criminal justice system, and while we may have an embarrassing legacy problem with the Guantánamo detainees, we will never go down that road again. We now know that—in the platitudinous words of President Obama—we can simply "reject as false the choice between our safety and our ideals."[2] And if we just honor the latter, we can rest assured that the former will surely follow.

It's an argument that brings to mind the old Russian aphorism "Pray to God, but row to shore." I certainly hope that the United States never again finds itself in the position of having to fight non-uniformed combatants who attack U.S. interests and civilians from the safe environs of a failed state. I also hope that if that situation ever does arise again, we will by then have developed more foolproof methods of distinguishing between the enemy and both foreign relief workers and local shepherds. If not, I further hope that the enemy should at least be small and discrete enough that authorities can process all captures through the criminal justice system and thereby avoid all of these difficult questions. But hope must supplement, not replace, planning—in particular when the things that one hopes for seem so unlikely to materialize.

Anticipating the future of warfare is a parlor game that has made many a smart person look stupid in relatively short order, but one probably would not want to bet on even the short-term ability of the United States to avoid in the future the problems that led to Guantánamo and Bagram in only the recent past. Does anyone really believe that in its next great war the United States will see its forces arrayed along a front against the forces of another major state for any protracted period of time? While one can imagine such a scenario in the Taiwan Strait or the Korean Peninsula, that particular form of warfare is, generally speaking, on the decline. The nature of U.S. military power normally ensures that any such confrontation would either be deterred entirely by the threat of nuclear attack or would be over rather quickly—as were both recent confrontations with Saddam Hussein's Iraqi army.

What might not end quickly is the insurgency that might follow an overwhelming U.S. victory. And, as we have also learned, what might not end quickly is the effort to pacify the failed states from which nonstate groups will continue to attack us. Those are precisely the situations that have given rise to our current detention problem. And I, at least, would not bet against them as a harbinger of the future of U.S. warfare.

There are some obvious candidates for the next arena in which U.S. forces will confront irregular forces committed to violating the rules of warfare—Yemen, Somalia, and parts of Pakistan chief among them. But one doesn't have to have any special perspicacity to understand how foolish it is to assume that the next war will look *nothing* like the last two that the United States has fought in terms of the detention difficulties it will create. One simply needs to imagine that *some* such conflict seems at least plausible—if not, as I suspect, preponderantly likely. Once one accepts that argument, our society's failure to row for shore—to make even rudimentary legal plans for that day—seems utterly self-defeating.

Construct whatever scenario you like for this conflict. Use whatever country name suits you; Fredonia will do if you prefer something that doesn't end in "stan." Give the enemy whatever ethnic and religious background seems plausible; you can make it drug cartels and narco-terrorists in Colombia or Mexico if you want to change the subject from the West's confrontation with violent Islamism. On the other hand, if you prefer to take certain contemporary political conflicts to their logical conclusions, imagine that it's Iran—a country of 70 million people, at least some of whom would not welcome U.S. forces as liberators. The only thing that matters is that enemy forces are irregulars—hard to identify and easy to confuse with the civilians among whom they will hide—and that they will fight in the context of some ungoverned territory. What will happen?

For starters, U.S. forces will capture a bunch of people. The vast majority of those people will be fighters of one sort of another or people directly supporting the conflict, but our forces will, of course, overcapture as well. The need to protect our forces, the fog of war, and the blurry line between combatant and civilian in such conflicts will all conspire to generate a certain margin of error in which some random people will get mixed in with the bad guys. Everyone will know that that is happening—just as everyone knows that civilians get killed and injured in military attacks. Yet unlike collateral damage, wrongful detentions will bother us in an ongoing fashion.

That will not be an altogether irrational response. Though the injury done to someone accidently killed immeasurably exceeds the injury done to someone erroneously detained, the dead civilian is no *more* dead one year later than he was on the day of the errant strike. The injury is done, cannot be undone, and does not compound with time. By contrast, erroneous deprivation of liberty grows worse the longer that it goes on. It can be corrected, prospectively if not retrospectively. The victimization of the innocent detainee, though of a lesser order than that of the innocent person whom we kill, does pay compound interest. As a consequence, shortly after we begin capturing, we will as a society begin worrying.

Second, we will not avail ourselves of either of two mechanisms for relieving that worry. The criminal justice process will not be available, because the numbers of detainees will be too large and the evidence against many of them too poor, too impressionistic, and too probabilistic to support criminal cases. Importantly, however, we also will not avail ourselves of the out that the laws of war offer: treating all detainees as privileged belligerents or prisoners of war. We will not do that for exactly the same reasons that we have not done it in Afghanistan—one practical and the other spiritual. At a practical level, the intelligence gathering exigencies of the conflict will require greater flexibility in interrogating detainees than the Geneva Conventions tolerate for prisoners of war. At a spiritual level, we will not want to afford the captives any kind of honorable status. The United States has never gone along with the rest of the world's decision to treat irregulars who fight by no known rules as the equivalent of honorable soldiers, and I have trouble imagining that it will begin to do so.

Third, there will be no government ready, willing, and able to assist us in handling the detainees. The very conditions that give rise to the conflict in the first place will ensure that there is no local government capable of helping. If one exists at all, it will be too weak, too corrupt, and too infiltrated by the bad guys to handle thousands or tens of thousands of detainees. European partners in the operation, meanwhile, will curiously abstain from this particular aspect of it. If they show up at all, they will show up to do the nice parts of the coalition project. They will leave all of the nastiest stuff to the United States—and detention will surely fall squarely in that category.

Fourth, as a consequence, U.S. forces will use whatever screening criteria they can cobble together—probably based on some combination of local conditions and the lessons learned in Iraq and Afghanistan. And they will end up making imperfect decisions as to whether to hold people based on the perceived threat that they pose at the time. Depending on how many detainees there are, how long we intend to hold them, and how good our information is, we may use a wide- or a fine-toothed comb. Either way, there will be errors in both directions.

And then, fifth, our forces will have to put the detainees somewhere. We know that they will not choose Guantánamo Bay, for precisely the same reason that the Bush administration *did choose* Guantánamo Bay: they will want to keep the detainees out of the reach of U.S. federal courts. If whatever legal doctrine then exists looks anything like current law, they will choose somewhere in the theater of combat. The case law, after all, now paradoxically makes habeas review more likely if detainees are removed from the theater and thus creates incentives to hold people in cruder, more dangerous theater facilities. They will have to choose a place that is operationally secure—somewhere the United States has near-total freedom of movement and answers to nobody else. And then, as night follows day, we will confront the question of whether the chosen facility really *does lie out of the reach of the courts.* We will earnestly ask ourselves whether it is more like the United States proper or more like Guantánamo (where the courts have jurisdiction), or more like Bagram (where the courts for now have no jurisdiction), or more like the Landsberg prison in Germany (where the courts had none in 1950). The longer we hold people, the more anxious we get about the compound interest that we are paying some of the detainees in injustice, and the more the waning of the conflict transforms serious threats into pathetic victims, the more we will second-guess our ad hoc choices and move the goal posts on ourselves.

We will, to lay the matter bare, have recreated Guantánamo. That is, we will have recreated the real Guantánamo—which is not the facility itself but the problems that gave rise to the facility, the problems that closing the facility will do nothing to address. Perhaps we will tolerate this new Guantánamo with greater equanimity than we did the first time; these things never traumatize one as much the second time around. Perhaps the world too will tolerate it a little more readily, particularly if we have at the key moment a Democratic president willing to beat his breast over the matter rather than a Republican president eager to thump his chest over it. But those are optical differences, not legal ones— and we shouldn't count on them. The point is that we will face exactly the same problems that we faced in the first decade of the war on terror, and we will face them again precisely because we refused to adequately address the questions that gave rise to them in the first place.

Denial has proven itself a more flexible tool for managing detentions than I would have believed possible. It has given the United States a relatively stable and reasonably favorable short-term equilibrium, one in which international pressure over detention matters has declined dramatically. That equilibrium, to be sure, has its costs—costs in lives, costs in intelligence, moral costs, and costs in coherence. But if one truly believed that the United States would never again face the problems that gave rise to our detention mess, one might reasonably conclude that the costs are worth paying.

Yet merely to state that belief is to falsify it. Whatever pose one strikes about living our values or restoring the rule of law, one simply cannot contend both confidently and honestly that Guantánamo, the CIA's secret prisons program, and the tens of thousands of noncriminal detentions that have taken place around the world flowed simply from post–September 11 fears and a lawless Bush administration. They resulted, in at least significant part, from the absence of clear answers to some fairly basic questions. While in many situations denial can serve to delegate the answering of those questions—for the lucky few to courts, for many more to proxy governments, and for the least lucky to the remote pilots of CIA drones—eventually delegation will let critical decisions slip through the cracks. And those cracks will, I fear, prove far wider that they appear at the moment.

5

The Case for Candor

No one seriously defends the current array of U.S. detention policies. The government, of course, defends individual policies against court challenges, but it also has fiercely resisted other elements of current policy prior to their judicial imposition. Human rights groups and lawyers for detainees admire some of the current elements of the array and challenge others as affronts to the rule of law. A great many people defend current policies as a tactical matter, believing that to open them up to renegotiation would make the situation worse than it already is. Many human rights and civil liberties activists, for example, acknowledge privately that in an ideal world the United States would treat these issues legislatively. They admit that their opposition to legislation reflects less a principled belief that the United States *should* ask its courts for the answers than a tactical judgment that the legislature is dangerous terrain for them. Congress will only make matters worse, they argue, by granting the government broad powers that will then have great legitimacy. Many government lawyers privately say more or less the same thing. On the other hand, elements of the Bush administration believed that they should rely on executive power for detention because Congress would slap intolerable restrictions on the president if given the chance. Yet almost nobody defends the current system, except in comparison to whatever system he or she fears more.

And why should anyone defend the status quo—as an intellectual matter, a policy matter, a legal matter, or a matter of common sense? Under what conceivable set of values would one admire a set of detention rules whose contours vary so wildly according to factors so unrelated to either liberty or security? Surely, no self-respecting human rights advocate, believing that the rule of law requires habeas corpus review of detentions for detainees held at Guantánamo, could regard with equanimity the total deprivation of judicial review for the many more detainees held elsewhere in the world. If one truly believes that habeas review is a fulcrum on which our values pivot, it beggars belief that one would find satisfying the notion that the rule of law hinges on the odd terms of the U.S. lease of Guantánamo. It also beggars belief that the government could evade the rule of law by holding detainees in *more dangerous conditions* instead of removing them from the arena of combat. Such a person must also feel at least modest discomfort at the increased reliance on proxy forces and Predator strikes that has accompanied the human rights victories over administration detention policies. Surely, such a person would regard the closure of Guantánamo—if it ever happens—as the most Pyrrhic of victories if it ends up meaning that future detainees, if captured at all, will be held somewhere else, somewhere darker, by forces less professional and less constrained by law than our own. The most that a self-respecting human rights activist could honestly say for the current situation is that it might represent the beginning of greater judicial oversight of international counterterrorism, the birth of a regime that will grow more comprehensive over time.

Those concerned primarily with security have no more reason to admire the current arrangements. They have no idea what conduct, legal and unreviewable today, will end up slapped down by the courts five years from now. They do not know how far what restrictions extend or where the trend toward judicialization will stop. The most that they can honestly say for the system is that it does not necessarily mean more trouble than a big bait-and-switch for a declining group of people at Guantánamo—where no new detainee will ever set foot. If the most that one can say from a human rights point of view is that the regime might get better, the most that one can say from a security point of view is that it might not get worse. Neither statement constitutes high praise.

I don't argue that candor can satisfy all sides. It can't. Some of these issues come perilously close to being zero-sum games—there will be losers if we handle detention openly and candidly; there will be losers if we don't. I would not, in other words, argue that we can better *balance* liberty and security with greater candor, serving all interests and reaching some happy medium that satisfies everyone. My argument is somewhat humbler than that. It's not that candor can help us arrange our affairs so that everyone wins; it's that it can help us arrange them so that everyone doesn't always lose—so that we do not have a system in which the refusal to make choices guarantees outcomes that undermine everyone's interests.

What would a policy based on candor look like? As a preliminary matter, it would dispense with the very marginal question of whether the detention site at Guantánamo Bay should stay or go. The location of a detention site is not now and has never been the important issue. The important issue concerns the rules for detention, the circumstances under which we will and will not detain people, and the rights that we are prepared to grant to those subject to whatever system we set up. President Obama and Senator McCain alike, by promising to close Guantánamo rather than to fix a floundering detention system, put the wrong policy issue at the center of the conversation. As long as it remains there, we will miss the larger picture. The truth is that whether Guantánamo shuts down or remains with us indefinitely matters only in terms of public relations. Closing it will not fix the policy problem, and leaving it open will not prevent us from forging a new detention policy. Making a fetish out of either closing it or keeping it only puts international and domestic focus on benchmarks that have nothing to do with the success of our detention operations. How many detainees remain at Guantánamo? On what date does the last one leave? Such questions reflect an instinct for the capillaries.

A policy based on candor would create distinctions between different categories of detainees, not between different categories of detention facilities. Detention rules that depend on geography create an irresistible temptation for the government to decide where to house a given detainee on the basis of which system of review it wishes to use for that person. Habeas corpus review too cumbersome in a particular case? Don't bring that detainee to Guantánamo or to the United States. This is a silly cat-and-mouse game. The relevant inquiry is what the government alleges against what sort of person, using what kind of evidence. If we write good rules for the different groups of people that we confront, sorting them into the right facilities in the right locations will not prove especially difficult.

Equally important, a candid policy would aim to *address* rather than to avoid the key questions whose answers drive the operation of the U.S. detention system. This system operates as an organism, not as a series of disconnected parts, and unless we treat it as a system, we will always discover later that the water has found a different route to the sea. The current bypassing of Guantánamo is one example of this, but there are many others. In 1996, Congress created the Alien Terrorist Removal Court to supervise the removal from the United States of aliens suspected of terrorist activity. You probably have never heard of it. Why? Because it has never convened to hear a single case. Not thinking about the system as a whole, Congress created rules for the court that were so much more generous to the accused than the rules governing the normal immigration system that since then the executive branch has always chosen to deport aliens suspected of being terrorists using the normal, permissive rules.[1]

Similarly, some of the most heated debates over the Patriot Act in 2001 concerned none of the surveillance issues on which society later focused but the power granted to the Attorney General to lock up aliens suspected of terrorism for seven days before filing immigration charges.[2] Yet once again, that power has never been invoked; it's so easy to lock up immigrants under other immigration authorities that it actually added little to the government's arsenal. Unless one considers the interactions of the many components of our complex detention system, one ends up not rationalizing the system but adding more layers of irrationality.

Broadly speaking, the United States is dealing with three overlapping categories of people in its global counterterrorism operations:

—criminal suspects, whose salient feature is their violation of federal criminal statutes

—fighters, who in some meaningful sense joined the military forces of the enemy and whose salient feature is belligerency under either international law or the AUMF

—hybrid figures, who display elements of both the criminal and the fighter, but whose ultimate salience is some combination of extreme dangerousness and high intelligence value.

Many detainees fall plausibly into more than one of these groups, and some fall into all three. There probably is no way to define as a matter of law the category in which a given detainee should go. Faced, for example, with a Khalid Sheikh Mohammed, the executive branch will inevitably face a choice of regimes: does it wish to treat him as a criminal suspect, a high-value intelligence target, an enemy belligerent, or all three at different times after his capture? What's more, for at least some fighters and hybrid figures—and arguably for quite a few—criminal law will offer the most effective means of intelligence gathering, long-term neutralization, or both. So decisions regarding which box to put a given detainee in will not always be governed by which seems the cleanest fit in a conceptual sense. Sometimes tactical exigencies will legitimately win out.

Still, there have to be rules for each major category of detainee—and they have to be clear, sensible, and known rules.

Right now, only the first category—the criminal suspect—has a clearly defined set of rules to govern his incarceration and the adjudication of his case. The rules governing detention of fighters are being contested in numerous Guantánamo habeas corpus cases, as we have seen, and in any event those rules vary significantly by geography. Meanwhile, there has been no serious effort whatsoever to establish distinct rules for detentions of individuals in the third category. Civil libertarians, human rights groups, and the political left insist on cramming this group of people into the category of criminal suspects; the political right insists on cramming it into the category of wartime detainees. The Obama and Bush administrations talked very differently about the group. The Bush administration talked in the language of war; the Obama administration has sometimes preferred the language of criminal justice. Yet each administration has drawn frequently on both the law of war and the criminal law—sometimes using one, sometimes the other. In truth, the individuals in the third group deeply stress both categories and properly require rules of their own.

It's not my intent to map out in detail here the sort of regimes that might better govern these three categories. I have done so elsewhere for those readers who are interested. My aim here is to sketch them, to describe the big picture—a broad public policy architecture that might address U.S. needs in a more rational fashion.

One can view the problem of designing this architecture through many lenses. In common debate, we tend to ask the too-crude question of whether to think of the conflict in terms of warfare or law enforcement when both obviously play a role. In a related fashion, we can ask what authorities and detention powers we want the various components of the U.S. government to have, assuming that the government will use all of the tools that we give it. In my opinion, two lenses offer especially useful and illuminating views of the subject.

The first lens focuses on the people—that is, on the category of detainee in question. The idea is to conceptualize the broad project at hand as one of defining the rules concerning how U.S. forces of various types should handle each of the three major groups described above. By doing so, we can hope to define better both the borders between the groups and our working understanding of the proper way to handle each.

We might begin by focusing on the first group: criminal suspects. The criminal law is the most developed of our relevant legal systems. Its capacity to handle terrorist suspects fairly and constitutionally has proven far greater than imagined by many commentators—particularly conservatives—in the wake of September 11. In the years since, we have significantly enhanced the system in a number of respects—particularly with regard to the conduct that it now forbids by non–U.S. nationals operating overseas and at relatively early stages of potential operations.

In cases in which we can use it effectively, the criminal justice apparatus has certain undeniable advantages over all of the alternatives to it. It offers the most legitimate and secure legal basis for imposing long-term detention. It sometimes, although by no means consistently, also serves as an excellent device for intelligence gathering—particularly when attorneys for the accused, faced with overwhelming evidence against their clients, can help convince them that cooperation offers their only hope for leniency. As Assistant Attorney General David Kris put it, "The fact is, when the government has a strong prosecution case in an Article III court, the defendant knows this, and he knows that he will spend a long time in a small cell, which creates powerful incentives for him to cooperate with us, not that those incentives always produce cooperation, just that, in the run of cases, they do . . . that quite a bit."[3]

The system's major disadvantages involve its limited capacity with respect to processing large numbers of detainees. It works best when dealing with small numbers, and using it as a mechanism for processing sudden influxes of hundreds or thousands of detainees is inconceivable. Its legitimacy comes from the care with which it considers the evidence of each element of each offense alleged against each captive, a feature that makes it far too labor intensive and evidence intensive to handle huge volumes of detainees. Still, for periods in which the number of captives remains low—periods in which U.S. combat forces can rely on well-developed proxies for overseas detentions—the justice system can and will bear a great deal of the weight. That is by and large a good thing, as its use oftentimes achieves the best balance of society's many interests in a detention. That said, the system is far from perfect, and its use often has real costs and dangers. If there exist ways to augment its capacity and to allow it to handle a greater percentage of captives more comfortably, that could both minimize controversy and maximize the effectiveness of what is, in many instances, the most effective system.

At the same time, recognizing that it's unlikely that we have captured our last large contingent of fighters abroad, we also need to develop strong legislative authorization for—and regulation of—the sort of military detentions that our conflicts now require. To the extent that we think of such fighters as traditional captures under the laws of war, we have a relatively developed system for dealing with them too: the military can lawfully hold them until the termination of hostilities, although it often chooses to release them first or transfer them to foreign custody. As almost everyone recognizes, however, this system is significantly underdeveloped for processing large numbers of hard-to-identify captives who operate out of uniform and who tend to deny their affiliations with the enemy.

The capacity for error in both detentions and releases is higher with respect to non-uniformed fighters than in conventional law-of-war detentions, and the traditional instruments for separating combatants from civilians are too crude. The Bush administration recognized that and implemented new procedures at Guantánamo. The Obama administration extended those procedures—or something very much like them—to Bagram. The Supreme Court, at least with respect to Guantánamo, insisted on the even-more-exacting instrument of habeas review (though how exacting, as we have seen, is still being worked out by the courts). To put it bluntly, a political consensus of sorts has developed that we need to adapt the traditional military detention power for use in conflicts with actors who disrespect the most basic premises of the Geneva Conventions. We argue over the type of adaptation—with everything from relatively minimal procedures to full-blown habeas review very much on the table. But nobody argues any more that military detentions in this conflict will or should involve the same fact-finding instruments that we use for the prisoner of war in a foreign army. This consensus has actually existed for years, yet we have nonetheless resisted developing the sort of legal architecture that embodies it. Doing so, after all, involves making hard choices. Does holding captives who are each likely—but not certain—to be a part of enemy forces disquiet us more than releasing them? How much evidence, proven to whom and under what conditions, will we define as sufficient? Those questions lack obvious answers. It is far easier for people across the political spectrum to refuse to entertain them, with those on the right drawing simplistic analogies between the current conflict and those that have come before it and those on the left denying that military detention has any place in our current struggles at all. A policy based on candor would deny the political system the luxury of such complacency and insist on addressing the major questions before the next big influx of detainees, so that we make and debate our choices in the open and hold ourselves accountable for them.

Finally, a policy based on candor would address directly the third category of detainees, the hybrid captives. Depending on how one handles the first two categories, it may be possible to avoid writing specific laws for this group. If, for example, one writes greater flexibility into the criminal justice system and also creates a stable architecture for military detention that includes the authority to hold people acting on behalf of the enemy far from an obvious battlefield, one might subsume this category of detainee into the other two. I suspect that that is not a good idea, but it is a possibility. It is not possible, by contrast, to avoid considering this category in the overall design of the detention system as a whole. Such captives are, after all, relatively numerous, and they present society with enormously high stakes. The group includes, almost by definition, the highest-value captives that U.S. forces take, and they will stress whatever system one tries to cram them into. We need to think through how we will handle them and at least consider designing rules that govern their detentions specifically.

Another lens through which to view the broad problem examines a slightly different set of questions, focused less on the categories of detainees than on the categories of *situations* in which we use detention in one form or another. Looking at the matter this way, we would first need to decide how we wish to handle the legacies of our earlier detention policies—that is, the remaining detainees at Guantánamo and Bagram. That is actually more than one question, since the legal regimes at the two facilities are quite different and will remain so as long as the courts assert habeas jurisdiction over one but not over the other. That said, a single big problem does lie beneath all of the various legacy detention issues: How do we want to handle people detained under the laws of war during an early phase of a conflict that looks very different today? What sort of judicial and administrative procedures do we want to impose retroactively on detentions that we inaugurated with an altogether different set of rules and assumptions in mind?

To avoid facing the same problem the next time around, we should think through how in the future we want to handle people similar to those who now present us with this legacy problem. When we have the opportunity to take future captives into custody, how do we avoid repeating the bait-and-switch that we have engineered for ourselves? How do we avoid capturing people and justifying their initial detention based on crude intelligence, imagining ourselves to be operating within a relatively conventional law-of-war framework, and then finding our allies, our courts, and our own consciences pushing us toward applying a much higher set of standards down the road?

That question presents itself rather differently if one imagines large instead of small numbers of captives, and the answer also probably varies depending on which detainees we imagine as our prototypes. Guantánamo, after all, involved an enormous range of people—people that we probably should not have thrown together and treated as a single group in the first place—and we would do well to avoid throwing such people together in the future.

We also need to address crisis situations. How do we want to handle crisis detentions in the future, both at home and abroad? How do we want to treat the suspect whom the FBI pulls off of an airplane with his underwear on fire? How do we want to treat the people captured in a joint operation by the CIA and some foreign intelligence service in a safe-house raid aimed at a high-value target? The system or systems for the latter situation need to be flexible enough to process not only the high-value target—about whom we may know a great deal and on whom we may have a lot of evidence—but also the unnamed people who surround him, about whom we may know nothing.

Whichever lens one uses, a common set of tasks emerges:

—We need to optimize our criminal justice capacity, in particular in order to manage better the domestic crisis detention scenario.

—We need a societal agreement concerning the handling of the legacy detentions.

—We need to establish procedures for future law-of-war detentions that will create sensible review mechanisms, whether judicial or administrative, rather than arbitrarily apply an especially probing habeas regime in some detainees' cases but not in others.

—We need to decide how we want to handle hybrid detainees, particularly in a crisis environment.

In many respects, optimizing the criminal justice system to handle counterterrorism cases is the easiest of these tasks. We have honed the rules of criminal law over hundreds of years into an especially well-defined and well-elaborated organism. Many of its rules are constitutional in nature—making them all but impossible to amend. While one can, of course, criminalize more behaviors and adjust procedural rules to a certain degree, the system itself is, in the main, what it is. Its comparatively fixed quality makes imagining dramatic changes to its capacity difficult; no conceivable rule change, for example, will allow it to process a sudden influx of detainees like those captured in Afghanistan in the early years of U.S. counterterrorism efforts there. On the other hand, it makes those reforms that are possible somewhat easier to envisage. Refining an existing system is a simpler task than building one from scratch or rehabbing one completely.

Conservatives often gripe at the use of the criminal justice system as a counterterrorism instrument. They are wrong to do so. It is not nearly as backward-looking as they sometimes imagine. While it cannot handle all legitimate detainees, as many civil libertarians and human rights advocates would like it to, it does offer a powerful frontline system for nearly all domestic captures. This system has the capacity not only to punish terrorists for attacks after they take place but also to punish those planning or plotting attacks or engaging in any activities that constitute active support of terrorist groups. What's more, the system's coercive pressures are so extreme—including the threat of death sentences and lifetime confinement in supermax prisons—that it often offers excellent intelligence gathering opportunities.

What it cannot offer, however, is *consistent* opportunities for intelligence gathering. A system that guarantees one the right to remain silent will encourage some captives to remain silent. A system that insists on early legal representation for detainees will find that interrogations are influenced not only by lawyers who encourage cooperation from their clients but also by some who encourage reticence. A system that resolves disputes through litigation can often delay cooperation and intelligence collection until protracted negotiations and litigation come to resolution. While the criminal justice system often facilitates interrogation, in short, it is not designed chiefly to facilitate interrogation, so in the crisis detention setting, a measure of doubt will exist regarding the role that it will play with respect to intelligence gathering.

While to a great degree this problem is inherent in the system, relatively small changes could make it at least somewhat less acute. Most important, Congress could try to give authorities a bit of a grace period in domestic crisis detentions, a block of time in the immediate aftermath of a high-stakes capture in which to interrogate a suspect without taking him before a magistrate. We tend to argue over the rules that govern the first few hours and days of criminal detention in the language of *Miranda,* with conservatives complaining that the reading of rights early in an interrogation risks compromising intelligence gathering in the name of legal niceties. But the question of when law enforcement authorities inform a suspect of his rights is far from the biggest problem that they face. Most suspects who talk do not stop talking because an FBI agent ritualistically at some point recites the rights that the suspect has so often heard recited in television shows. The more serious obstacle is the requirement that authorities bring the suspect before a judicial officer almost immediately. That formal proceeding interrupts the interrogation and sets in motion procedures that can, under certain circumstances, prevent it from restarting. Even if the courts will not later admit all of the suspect's statements as evidence against him, a grace period within the criminal justice system in which investigators might interrogate someone uninterrupted would relieve to some extent the dual pressures that the executive branch now faces in crisis detentions—the need to maximize its intelligence take without compromising its criminal case.

Threading this needle within existing doctrine is a tricky matter, but it should be possible. The Supreme Court has never specified the outer limit on the period within which authorities can hold a suspect in a national security emergency without bringing him before a judge or letting him meet with a lawyer. While federal rules and statutes require that a suspect appear before a magistrate within a "reasonable" period of time and statements given after more than a six-hour delay in presentment are generally not admissible, the government does not run into presumptive constitutional difficulties for forty-eight hours over the detention itself. It merely risks losing the ability to use the suspect's statements as evidence against him if those statements are given after the reasonable period has elapsed. What's more, the Supreme Court has never confronted a well-crafted statutory scheme that authorizes delaying presentment only in the narrow context of an unfolding national security emergency. If such a scheme were designed carefully and not abused, it's hard for me to imagine that the Court would not uphold it.

The contours of such a system could be relatively simple. In a crisis detention, the government could seek permission from a judge to delay presentment for, say, a small, specified number of days with high-level political certification both that there exists probable cause for believing that a terrorist crime has been or may be committed and that the suspect has information critical to national security. Congress also could try to create a presumption that unwarned statements given within the grace period are not per se out of bounds in terms of later admissibility—although the longer the unwarned, lawyerless detainee is held, the less the courts will be inclined to respect that presumption. It is a striking fact that a great many countries that face serious terrorism problems have some kind of detention grace period for crises. It is not hard to imagine that Congress might give the executive branch similar latitude within the U.S. criminal justice system.

Indeed, it is just barely possible that Congress will do that. The Obama administration has publicly toyed with the idea of seeking such a law in response to the Times Square and Christmas

Day bombing attempts. The Justice Department has tended to talk about the matter less as a detention question than as an effort to reform the *Miranda* rule—or, more precisely, to expand and codify the public safety exception to the *Miranda* rule. But the two issues are inextricably linked, and the *Miranda* question is, of the two, by far the less important. Legislation in this area will become more likely the more that crisis detention incidents occur and the more that they take place in circumstances in which detainee cooperation does not materialize quickly and its absence forces the government to choose between vital interrogation interests and the preservation of its criminal case.

One should not, however, overstate the likely impact of any legislation in this area. Any grace period apt to survive constitutional scrutiny will be short—measured in days, not weeks or months. And the enemy can train to handle and resist a short, defined period of intensive interrogation. What's more, in a number of cases, including that of Shahzad, the accused in the Times Square bombing attempt, suspects have already waived the right to early presentment, creating by default the very grace period that such a law would create statutorily. The importance of this change lies less in the additional operational flexibility that it would create in certain cases than in the definition for American legal and political culture of a distinct and legitimate set of standard procedures for high-stakes terrorism cases—procedures tailored to optimize the government's competing vital concerns. Giving authorities such a tool should alleviate the pincer action under current law, whereby the administration now faces harsh criticism and second-guessing however it chooses to treat a suspect.

The time window for the second task—coming to some sort of agreement concerning the legacy detainees—is fast closing. The efforts of the past and current administrations alike to depopulate Guantánamo have reduced its denizens to a relatively small handful whose habeas corpus cases are now winding their way through the court system. This process, as we have seen, is writing its own rules, however haphazardly, and resolving the status of the detainees at issue, however imperfectly. Meanwhile, the lower courts have clarified for now that they have no jurisdiction over Bagram, control of which the military means to transfer gradually to Afghan authorities in any event. So the detainees there—comparatively invisible, anyway—will at some point disappear in a puff of smoke altogether, at least as a problem for U.S. detention policy. One might reasonably ask whether it really is important at this late stage for Congress to resolve the legacy problem or whether, having passed the buck for so many years, it might as well let other institutions finish the job that it sloughed off on them.

But sighing in resignation and accepting that the courts will write the rules for Guantánamo ignores two important ways in which the legacy and the future are bound up with one another. First, leaving the courts to resolve Guantánamo works only if one can rest very assured that the habeas regime established for Guantánamo really will stay at Guantánamo. In the wake of the D.C. Circuit's strong refusal to extend habeas to Bagram, that assumption seems reasonable for the immediate term. In my view, however, it is as unlikely to hold in the long run as the courts were unlikely in the first place to tolerate Guantánamo's lying outside of their purview forever. I don't purport to know how long it will take. But it seems to me that the next time the United States locks up a large group of people at a site chosen because of its inaccessibility to the courts and proceeds to hold that group of people for a long, even indefinite, period of time, the courts will grow as anxious as they did last time. And the legal doctrine that insists that they keep their hands off the matter will be weaker than it was the last time—when it proved, despite being unequivocal, that it was not up to the task of keeping the courts away.

In other words, I suspect that the Guantánamo habeas cases will not be a historical blip, an event in legal history that took place in response to the unique nature of a particular base and the special affront to some sensibilities created by the activity in which a particular administration engaged there. It will instead turn out to be the beginning of judicial supervision of certain overseas detention activity, supervision that will grow over time, not shrink. If one expects it to develop in that direction or even acknowledges the possibility that it will, the current habeas cases take on importance not merely as a means of handling the Guantánamo legacy but as the core of that nascent system. The question then becomes whether or not we want to develop the core of that system in this incremental, ad hoc fashion or in one that is more actively legislative in character.

Second, as I mentioned earlier, a more immediate relationship exists between the habeas decisions and future detentions: the Mark Martins problem. The habeas courts, after all, are not simply deciding the fate of the detainees before them. They are interpreting the substantive law that governs the conflict—most important, the AUMF. Their opinions are, therefore, potentially important sources of law even in areas that they do not directly control. If a court finds that the military cannot detain a given person because the AUMF does not reach that person, that raises a serious question with regard to whether the military can take a similar person far afield into custody. It raises no less of a question regarding whether it can target such a person in a combat setting. As those cases work their way up the appellate ladder and become more binding as precedent, some of them may acquire profound importance for future detentions and targeting rules—even if detention and targeting questions never come before a habeas court. At a very basic level, these cases are going to define what it means to be part of the enemy and what sort of evidence proves that relationship. These are not questions that matter only in retrospect or that any legislature concerned with the overall architecture of the U.S. detention system should delegate to the courts.

The question at the molten core of these cases is, in general terms, easy to state: how convincing does the government have to be, using what sort evidence, to convince a judge that a given person is in some meaningful sense part of the enemy and that the judge should therefore uphold his potentially indefinite detention? The courts to date have shown little consistency in ruling on that bedrock question and the constituent questions that make it up, and no self-respecting legislature should, in any event, willingly cede the authority to answer those questions to anyone else.

Some of the judges have openly stated that they could use more guidance. In announcing his decision in one detainee's case, for example, Judge Thomas Hogan said from the bench that "it is unfortunate, in my view, that the Legislative Branch of our government, and the Executive Branch have not moved more strongly to provide uniform, clear rules and laws for handling these cases," and he called for a "national legislative solution with the assistance of the Executive so that these matters are handled promptly and uniformly and fairly for all concerned."[4] Similarly, in concurring with the D.C. Circuit's first decision in a habeas merits case, Judge Janice Rogers Brown wrote that "the circumstances that frustrate the judicial process are the same ones that make this situation particularly ripe for Congress to intervene pursuant to its policy expertise, democratic legitimacy, and oath to uphold and defend the Constitution. These cases present hard questions and hard choices, ones best faced directly."[5]

Facing those questions directly means that Congress must address head on a series of elemental issues that will come before habeas courts in any military detention case—questions that must guide military detention even when cases never come near a courtroom. The most important of them are the following:

—What is the substantive scope of the government's detention authority—that is, what sort of person falls within the category of individuals that the government may lock up under its power to wage war against al Qaeda and the Taliban? Does this class include only members of enemy forces or also their supporters? Can one even distinguish between the two? If the government is allowed to detain supporters, will any support qualify a person for detention or does it have to be substantial support? If the government can prove that a person has the requisite connection to the enemy, must it also prove that he is likely to commit a dangerous act of some description if released?

—Can a detainee sever his relationship with enemy forces in such a way that his detention is no longer a legal option? If a detainee once joined al Qaeda, does he always count as an al Qaeda member for legal purposes? Or can he leave the group after some period of membership or association and thus no longer qualify for detention? Can he break with the group *after capture* by cooperating with authorities and thereby no longer qualify for continued detention? If a detainee can sever his relationship with the enemy, who has the burden of showing that he did or did not do so? Does the detainee have to prove vitiation of the relationship or does the government have to prove its ongoing vitality?

—What presumptions should the courts make regarding government evidence? Should they grant government evidence a presumption of either authenticity or accuracy? Or, conversely, should they take the uncertainty and rough and tumble of warfare as a reason to treat government evidence whose provenance may be inexact with particular skepticism?

—What evidentiary rules should apply in these detention adjudications? How should the courts handle hearsay evidence or intelligence reports whose sources the government may not identify? How should they handle statements by a detainee's fellow prisoners in interrogations years ago when those witnesses may have long since left Guantánamo? How should they handle statements made by the detainees themselves under interrogation?

—How should the courts handle detainee or witness statements alleged to have been extracted involuntarily or through abuse? Who bears the burden of proving that a statement either was or was not given voluntarily? What level of coercion suffices to render a statement unusable in these proceedings? Where coercion has taken place, under what circumstances does it taint detainees' future statements and under what circumstances does the taint lift?

These are not questions that have correct or incorrect answers; they are questions that demand choices that, in turn, allocate risk. While the Constitution and international law bind the answers to some degree, the range of choices available is actually rather broad. One can make a compelling case for more or less restrictive detention rules. It is likely that the military and intelligence communities could learn to operate in a more restrictive detention environment than they have come to expect when operating overseas. There is no good argument, however, for deliberately maintaining incoherent and ill-defined rules that are constantly in flux, rules that the military and U.S. intelligence agencies cannot easily train soldiers to follow and that offer no safe harbor for executive conduct.

In August 2010, Senator Lindsey Graham introduced legislation that would begin to address some of these questions.[6] The difficulty that he has had in bringing together a coalition for such a bill highlights the paralysis that denial induces. The left views Graham's bill (on which I have advised his staff) suspiciously, as a preventive detention law. The right is no less suspicious, seeing it as a compromise measure that would facilitate the closure of Guantánamo, to which conservatives have, as discussed, developed a peculiar philosophical attachment. The administration, meanwhile, is frozen like a deer in the headlights, unable either to embrace the bill or to repudiate it. The most serious legislative effort to date on detention has not even warranted an answer from the president.

The third task—establishing the ground rules for future law-of-war detentions—ought to spark no special controversy. After all, almost everyone agrees that *some* detention is appropriate in at least *some* counterterrorism operations, if only in those that most resemble conventional military operations on an obvious battlefield in a zone of acknowledged military hostilities. As I have explained, both U.S. and international laws governing such detentions are woefully underdeveloped. The Geneva Conventions require only that the detaining party convene a "competent tribunal" if there is doubt about a captive's entitlement to treatment as a prisoner of war—or, presumably, about his identification as a combatant. The scope of the government's detention authority and the contours of the review mechanisms remain, years into the conflict, utterly undefined—or, rather, defined only in administrative procedures and regulations.

This arrangement offers flexibility, and that is nothing to sneeze at. Detention in Afghanistan, after all, differs from detention in Iraq. Detention when one has competent, reliable proxies differs from detention when one does not. Detention review mechanisms adequate for holding people for short periods of time may be wildly insufficient for holding people long term. Conversely, review mechanisms that give adequate attention to evidence to justify long-term detentions can encumber forces too much to use for en masse short-term detentions. One does not want a one-size-fits-all detention model for the military. The value of vagueness is that it permits agility. And whatever regime Congress might put in place will need to permit considerable agility too.

But vagueness has its own problems, a lack of legitimacy chief among them. When the government detains people for long periods of time without clear and specific legislative authorization to do so, it invites public anxiety, both domestic and international. Yes, it can rely on broad language like that in the AUMF and the Geneva Conventions, and in the short term nobody will make too much of a fuss. Over the long term, however, it inevitably will face questions about the ongoing relevance of those instruments to its activity. The authorization's language, as the conflict progresses and evolves, will inevitably cover detainees less obviously than it did at the outset, and the question of how long it authorizes detention will inevitably grow more acute.

That the AUMF says not a word about detention and the Geneva Conventions—so rich in their elaboration of the rights of POWs—say so little about the treatment of unprivileged belligerents forces the government to rely on the drafters' silence as permission to do things that they plainly did not imagine. The drafters of the Third Geneva Convention did not think about a global war against a nonstate actor who knows no rules and dons no uniform, and the Congress that hastily wrote the AUMF wasn't thinking about how much detention, and of whom, it wanted to permit. So they did not forbid—and that constitutes a permission of sorts, to be sure. But the longer a detention goes on, the louder the unsaid words seem to speak. And eventually, they truly undermine the legitimacy of the project. That is a big part of what happened at Guantánamo, where even the most unambiguously lawful detentions became disreputable. The many calls for the facility's closure were not just calls to free those wrongly detained; they were calls to abandon the project itself. Detention, in short, is not a matter of use it or lose it; it is a matter of defend it or lose it. If Congress will not stand clearly behind the propriety of long-term military detentions in some circumstances, those detentions will at some point suffer a major legitimacy crisis.

Standing behind detentions does not mean simply passing a series of laws to keep the courts out of them—as Congress tried to do with Guantánamo. It means explicitly authorizing detentions under the circumstances in which we want U.S. forces to engage in them. Given the very real operational need for flexibility in overseas military operations, such a law should not attempt to elaborate a detailed set of procedures. Rather, it should be a simple affair: a declarative statement that the executive branch is authorized under the AUMF and its successor instruments to take and detain prisoners who are part of or operating on behalf of the enemy's military forces. It should instruct the executive branch to write procedures to govern detentions under its terms and set the broad parameters for those procedures with respect to short- and long-term detentions. It should, in other words, frankly and directly authorize the activity in which the United States has engaged for the past nine years and in which we all expect it to engage for the foreseeable future: capturing and holding the enemy while engaged in that portion of global counterterrorism operations overseas that most clearly partakes of the quality of armed military conflict. We should think of such a law as nothing more than implementing legislation for the Third and Fourth Geneva Conventions as applied to a novel problem that the conventions' drafters did not anticipate and therefore did not address.

The Graham proposal contains the nucleus of such a law, although it does not fully develop the idea. It reiterates that the United States remains at war, and it contains an explicit statement that, in the context of this conflict, Congress authorizes the detention of the enemy.[7] Were the bill enacted, that statement would mark significant progress. Congress should, however, ultimately go further, to spur and legitimize the creation of the adjudicative structures necessary to manage such detentions.

Finally, there is the fourth task, the writing of rules for the hybrid detainee. The controversy here is easier to understand than the controversy over future law-of-war detentions. At least in theory, members of the hybrid class will nearly always also fall within either the criminal or law-of-war detention groups. Explicit detention authority for hybrid detainees therefore will necessarily duplicate preexisting powers to lock such people up— powers that, if Congress were to act responsibly with respect to the criminal and wartime detention categories, would rest on stronger ground to start with than they do now. One could imagine how sufficiently improving the other two categories might obviate the need for separate authority for the hybrid cases.

I do not doubt that with enough creativity and will we could cram hybrid detainees into the other two categories. Candor, however, would have us do otherwise. We detain these people not because they have committed crimes or because they are soldiers for the other side in a conflict, but because they are really dangerous people, sworn to attack us, who are deeply knowledgeable about plans to do just that. We hold them both to incapacitate and to interrogate—and those needs may persist for some time. During that time, criminal prosecution and the demands of the rigorous systems that facilitate it can sometimes encumber more important objectives. Authorities may not have sufficient evidence—or sufficient admissible evidence—to prosecute the people in this category, particularly those captured abroad. In some cases, they may not wish to acknowledge publicly even that they have captured the person. In some cases, as in raids on safe houses, they may not know much at first about some of the people in custody. As a practical matter, a legal system that does not directly confront hybrid detainees encourages the use of proxies. It is a notable fact that in 2002 and 2003 Pakistani forces turned major captives over to U.S. forces because we preferred to have them and the Pakistanis preferred to get them off their hands. Now our forces leave major captives with the Pakistanis.

In 2009, writing with a lawyer named Colleen Peppard, I attempted to draft a model law that would more optimally govern hybrid detentions. The model law, as we envisioned it, was designed to provide significant benefits to both detainees and the government. The government could invoke it at its discretion in lieu of holding a noncitizen in law-of-war detention or filing criminal charges against him. If it did so, the detainee would receive timelier, more probing, and more frequent federal court review than he gets under the current habeas regime, where he waits years for review if held at Guantánamo or in the United States and gets no judicial review at all if the government holds him in theater. From the government's point of view, invoking the model law would serve to insulate law-of-war detentions from federal court review by removing the detention cases most likely to make adverse law—those involving suspects captured far from overt hostilities—to a federal court, which proceeds on more certain, better-defined grounds. And critically, it would implicate the judiciary in detentions from the outset, not involve them only years later, after prolonged detention has eroded the urgency of the decision to incapacitate a suspect.[8]

Current habeas review of detentions proceeds, loosely speaking, on an administrative law model. The executive branch uses its internal procedures to decide whether detainees are properly held. The detainee then challenges his detention, and habeas litigation—often years later—reviews the designation. The judge who hears such a case had no involvement in the initial detention decision, which often was made with only a limited sense of how robustly it would later stand up in federal court. Thus, when the court finally confronts a detention, the record tends to be weak and the elapsed time long, and the judiciary has no investment in its integrity. That structure differs significantly from other preventive detention judgments supervised by American courts—for the seriously mentally ill, for sex offenders, and for those detained prior to a trial, for example. Under those regimes, the judicial system *authorizes* the detention at the front end, rather than reviewing its propriety at the back end.

The goal of the model law was to bring terrorist detentions into line with this more sensible approach. As a result, it placed judicial review *at the outset* of a long-term detention and forced the government to go through that review again and again on a regular basis as long as the detention persisted. We designed the law that way to serve several purposes. First, it would clarify for the executive branch that it is speaking to a federal court from the very opening of a detention case. The executive branch, in other words, would not need merely to satisfy itself that it had the right guy; it would have to satisfy a judge. Second, it would implicate the judiciary in the detention decision from the beginning. The appellate courts would not be asked to defer to executive discretion in approving a detention but to defer to a considered set of factual findings by a federal district court judge. The result, as we envisioned it, would be both more professional collection and presentation of evidence by the government and less of a tendency on the part of the judiciary to move the goal posts.

In brief summary, the model law would allow the executive branch a fairly liberal initial detention authority, one useful in the short term for the disruption of terrorist plots, that would grow significantly more rigorous if the government decided to seek longer-term incapacitation of a detainee. Once the president identified a non-U.S. person whom he reasonably believed to pose an "imperative threat to security," the proposal would authorize him to detain that person for up to fourteen days before seeking judicial authorization for further detention. That detention period would cover both domestic plots like the Christmas Day bombing attempt and overseas captures like, say, that of a high-value Taliban or al Qaeda figure. We intended the initial period of detention to be a grace period, both to allow the executive branch to disrupt terrorist activity and to facilitate evidence collection and consultation between U.S. and foreign intelligence services for purposes of criminal prosecution, transfer to foreign custody, or longer-term detention. With the fourteen-day period, the president would be entitled to hold the individual without publicly disclosing his apprehension to facilitate the apprehension of associates or other actions that might be frustrated should news of the capture leak out to confederates.

Under the proposal, if the president sought to continue to detain the individual beyond the initial fourteen-day period, he would petition the U.S. District Court for the District of Columbia to issue a detention order under the authority that the model law would grant it. The proposal lays out an elaborate set of due process protections that would kick in at that point—protections in many respects more significant than those offered in the current habeas process. If the district court approved the president's petition, the court would issue an order authorizing the president to detain the individual for up to six months. That process could be repeated every six months until the president or the court determined that the individual no longer met the criteria established in the law or until the government referred the individual for trial, released him, or transferred him to foreign custody.

I mention the model law here not as the only possible solution to the problem of hybrid detainees but as one possible approach—an approach that would add due process protections to what detainees now receive and add enormous clarity and certainty to future government efforts to incapacitate the most dangerous captives. Others have advanced thoughtful ideas based on different underlying judgments. The broad point is simply that we pay a huge price for refusing to tailor our detention system to the purposes to which we are putting it. Writing rules specifically to govern the cases of hybrid detainees could reduce that price.

Ironically, a policy based on candor might end up having a certain amount in common with our current policy. For example, as U.S. forces gain confidence in the government of Iraq or of Afghanistan, they might—as they in fact already have done—turn over large numbers of prisoners to it, on the theory that managing the country's own nationals is one of the sovereign functions for which the United States wishes the country to take responsibility. While that might look rather like proxy detention, the difference would be that the transfers would be a vote of confidence in Afghan and Iraqi capacity, not a reflection of declining confidence in our own. A policy based on candor might sometimes even rely on proxy detention as a matter of convenience; however, it would never have to rely on it out of fear.

The argument for candor is, in the end, based on a simple proposition: detention is not a matter of shame but a tool of security and order that American law, for all our rhetorical handwringing, permits when truly necessary and when bounded by appropriate safeguards. That being the case, it makes no sense to pay the costs that a policy of denial extracts. We should have the courage to look at ourselves in the mirror and ask the simple question of when we truly need detention, and of what sort. And we should ask ourselves what safeguards are appropriate given our detention needs.

6

Conclusion

In both liberal and conservatives circles, a certain confusion reigns regarding whether fundamentally the Obama administration's legal policies in counterterrorism matters reflect continuity with or change from those of the Bush administration. The confusion gives rise to a kind of dualism in the way that both broad political movements talk about the question. The liberal side, in its more exuberant moments, boasts that Obama has restored the rule of law, banned torture, declared the closure of Guantánamo, and moved to reclaim America's moral leadership in the world. Yet having said those things, the same liberal voices have to mumble some uncomfortable admissions: Guantánamo remains open, and its population is declining no faster than it was during the Bush years; in any event, Bagram remains what Guantánamo was. We still have military commissions. We still do warrantless wiretapping. The government still asserts the state secrets privilege to frustrate certain types of national security litigation. The Obama administration has actually ramped up the use of Predator drones to kill suspected enemies and has all but publicly declared that it reserves the right to go after a U.S. citizen under certain circumstances. And while the Obama administration has closed the CIA's black sites and banned harsh interrogations, it hasn't moved to change the law governing such matters; the sites were empty anyway, the harsh interrogations, in practical terms at least, a thing of the past.

The conservative side speaks with a mirror-image dualism. Conservative commentators bemoan the new administration's supposed pre–September 11 law enforcement mentality. They thunder that the administration's laxity endangers the nation. Some have attacked the federal employment of lawyers who once represented Guantánamo detainees, implying—or sometimes outright alleging—that a fifth column of al Qaeda sympathizers is now running the government of the United States. Yet conservatives also turn around and wax triumphant at the signs of continuity—the continuation of noncriminal detention, for example—claiming vindication for the prior administration's policies in their adoption by its supposedly recklessly weak successor. "Obama is showing weakness," conservatives seem to be claiming. "He thinks he's fighting crime; he can't face that it's really war. And look, he's adopted all of our policies!" That line of argument brings to mind the joke Woody Allen tells at the outset of *Annie Hall*, in which he describes two old Jewish ladies at a Catskill mountain resort, one of whom complains to the other that the food is terrible. "Yeah, I know," her companion laments, "and such small portions!"

There is a reason that both broad political camps evince such confusion: the question of whether the advent of the Obama administration represents a break with or an institutionalization of the prior administration's policies actually is complicated. One gets a very different view of the matter depending on the axis along which one examines the question. If one looks at the substantive authorities that the two administrations have claimed, for example, one sees a great deal of continuity; by and large, the Obama administration hasn't forsworn the option of taking the muscular actions that its predecessor claimed the right to take. Detention is a good example of that continuity, although the trend covers far more than detention alone. On the other hand, if one looks instead at the legal theory under which the two administrations justified their actions, more discontinuity than continuity emerges. The Obama administration, unlike the Bush administration, does not make expansive claims of executive power but tends to rely more narrowly on the AUMF for its detention power. And the two administrations' rhetoric differs even more. The Bush administration engaged in a certain amount of chest thumping about its terrorism policies; the Obama administration sounds an apologetic note, always emphasizing the values that it shares with those discomfited by aggressive tactics, even when deploying those very tactics. The Bush administration insisted on the propriety of Guantánamo, even as it quietly transferred hundreds of detainees out of the facility. The Obama administration, in contrast, accedes to the facility's illegitimacy—indeed, insists that closing it is a national security imperative—even as it maintains it and defends the detentions there. In short, the picture looks very different depending on the aspect on which one focuses.

Yet among the few areas of undeniable and unambiguous continuity is that both administrations, for very different reasons, have embraced denial. For the Bush administration, denial was part of the insistence that September 11 had changed everything and that the United States was now at war. If one takes the war paradigm seriously, the president can simply exercise his war powers and the world can adjust. But the projects of making new rules and new legal structures, adapting criminal justice tools, and creating hybrid institutions all imply to some degree that the apparently bald, simple statement that the country is at war is actually complicated, textured, and difficult. For the Obama administration, denial has different roots—roots in a discomfort with legitimizing detention. This brand of denial finds its intellectual source in the sense that relying on the AUMF somehow disrupts American values less than does creating and elaborating new statutory systems for detention. The Bush administration feared that Congress would micromanage its detention power too aggressively if it opened the door, while the Obama administration fears the opposite: that Congress would recklessly vest in the executive the power to lock people up.

Yet if the sources of denial differ, the policies that have emerged from denial reflect remarkable continuity: both administrations have defended existing detentions, resisted encroachments of judicial jurisdiction beyond Guantánamo, reduced the detainee population, and avoided institutionalizing the authorities at issue in law. Denial has allowed both administrations to cling to some basic delusions. For the Bush administration, it was the delusion that the presidency had all the power that it needed. For the Obama administration, it's the delusion that the new administration is winding down the policies of the old rather than institutionalizing them for the long haul.

The war on terror has concurrently entered a strange phase—a phase in which relatively robust military efforts no longer produce large numbers of captives whom U.S. forces themselves have to hold. The war very much goes on, in many ways even accelerates, as do law enforcement operations targeting the same terrorist organizations. Yet the initial phase of the war, characterized by serial captures of large numbers of detainees, is over. That fact greatly facilitates the Obama administration's particular version of denial. It conditions us to expect that the problem of numbers was a Bush administration problem, that it will not arise again, and that the current task is merely to manage the last administration's mess—not to figure out how to manage the next such mess.

That attitude would make a certain amount of sense if we could be totally confident that this new phase were not merely a lull, that the Bush administration's mess were not a problem that will recur, perhaps repeatedly, as long as we lack the legal architecture to handle spasmodic influxes of detainees whose identities are uncertain.

I claim no expertise in forecasting geopolitics—and, indeed, harbor a certain suspicion of those who do. That said, I can imagine no especially compelling reason to believe that the problems that gave rise to our pitched political battles on detention are behind us. Rather, the prudent policymaker has to imagine that they will return, that inherent in large-scale overseas operations that are hybrids of military action and criminal investigation is the capture of people who neatly fit into no traditional detention category. The question that we face as a political and legal culture really boils down to whether we plan for this eventuality or whether we plan on never having to face it.

The American polity is not good at issues in which it is asked to make painful choices in the present by way of averting greater pain at some indeterminate point in the future. Few societies are. It is hard with respect to climate change and carbon emissions and with respect to national debt. And it is even harder with respect to writing rules that allow the government to deprive of liberty people that we have not yet captured—people that, we can tell ourselves, do not exist and that we will therefore never capture. While getting detention policy right does not involve any particular material sacrifice, it does involve some degree of spiritual sacrifice. It involves a measure of sacrifice of our civic mythology. It involves facing squarely the fact that our tradition is not as pure as we pretend and, perhaps more difficult still, that we do not want it to be. It involves making hard choices, choices that we would prefer not to make and that we have become adept at avoiding.

I am not one to insist that eventually the world will ineluctably resolve toward my conception of the good. It is not at all inevitable that we will make good choices in this area. As long as we keep capturing people, however, and keep having to decide what to do with them, it probably is inevitable that we will develop clearer rules and norms for handling them—whether good ones or bad ones. The question is whether we do so by lurching from crisis to crisis and seeing which of our approaches works best over time or whether we do so deliberately, by imagining the regimes that might govern the crises.

Over the last several years—under both the Bush administration and the Obama administration—we have seen a significant move toward a more deliberative, statutory approach to counterterrorism policy. After much Sturm und Drang over the National Security Agency's warrantless wiretapping program, Congress authorized it in law. Prodded by the Supreme Court, Bush went to Congress to get military commissions authorized, and Obama continued the trend by seeking a series of modest modifications to the Military Commissions Act. Bush signed the so-called McCain Amendment binding military personnel to the strictures of the Army Field Manual on interrogation, and Obama followed it up by requiring CIA as well as military personnel to follow the army rules. Across a range of areas and two ideologically distinct administrations, we have inched toward making more conscious decisions about what the rules should be.

Yet detention has remained the exception. That is not because it is less important; indeed, it is arguably the heart and soul of the legal disputes over U.S. counterterrorism policy. Only the Patriot Act predated it as a civil liberties concern in the wake of September 11, and at every moment since the outset of the current conflict, detention matters of one sort or another have had pride of place in the debate. Instead, detention has resisted resolution and institutionalization because it has taken on such spiritual importance. Early in Obama's presidency, Gregory Craig, then the White House counsel, told a journalist that "it's possible but hard to imagine Barack Obama as the first President of the United States to introduce a preventive-detention law."[1] As a factual matter, Craig's statement was, of course, inaccurate: Obama would not be the first if he did seek a preventive detention law. But the fact that Craig formulated the matter that way—as do many others, in and out of government—illustrates how fateful many people imagine the stakes to be. Somehow, long periods of inaction do not seem nearly so weighty. Yet they are no less fateful, and they too will produce some form of law of detention.

In its last few years in office, the Bush administration made a great investment in a Saudi rehabilitation program for jihadists, sending home the overwhelming majority of Saudi detainees. A few years later, the percentage of former detainees who have returned to the fight seems relatively low, though the exact numbers are fuzzy. That comparatively small number, however, includes a few who have gone on to leadership positions in a new terrorist group, al Qaeda in the Arabian Peninsula—the group responsible for the Christmas Day bombing attempt. So stunted is our debate over detention that we have no useful vocabulary for discussing whether that pattern represents a success or a failure. Assuming for a moment (probably counterfactually) that all of the Saudis that we released were properly detained, is it reasonable to keep 120 combatants locked up indefinitely to prevent two or three from doing something horrible that creates a new strategic threat for the United States? Conversely, is it irresponsible to take risks with civilian lives by releasing combatants who have some small percent chance of killing civilians? To avoid a serious debate about detention means to refuse to address such questions. It is not a morally serious position.

In addition, it leaves us especially vulnerable to recriminations after the fact. At the end of the film *The Usual Suspects*, to end where I began, the master criminal—who has pretended throughout the movie to be a cripple—limps out of the police station, his bad arm and hand stiff and useless. Down the street, the limp fades and the hand relaxes to normalcy, and he gets into his lawyer's car and drives off. Inside the police station, Agent Kujan comes to the blinding realization that he has been duped by a man who he thought was stupid but who had been selling him a bill of goods since they met. He races outside, but it is too late; the agent is left with only self-recrimination, frustration, and anger.

That is us, too, when former Guantánamo inmates turn out to be among the senior leadership of al Qaeda in the Arabian Peninsula. Yet unlike in the movie, which portrays Agent Kujan as the fool, we have no accountability when our system fails. Were these releases the fault of the courts (whose threats of review spurred them), the Bush administration (which carried them out), the Saudi government (which didn't keep track of former detainees adequately), or the left and the international community (which relentlessly pushed for them)? The less responsibility we take for detention, the less accountability there is when it goes wrong, as it most certainly will—when we lock up the wrong guys or release the wrong guys, when we jail Chinese Uighurs or release suicide bombers. It's long past time for us to face the reality of the project in which we are engaged.

Notes

Chapter One

1. Executive Order, "Review and Disposition of Individuals Detained at the Guantánamo Bay Naval Base and Closure of the Detention Facilities," January 22, 2009 (www.whitehouse.gov/the_press_office/Closure OfGuantanamoDetentionFacilities/).

2. Prepared Statement of Benjamin Wittes before the Senate Committee on the Judiciary, *Improving Detainee Policy: Handling Terrorism Detainees within the American Justice System*, 110 Cong., 2 sess., June 4, 2008 (http://judiciary.senate.gov/hearings/testimony.cfm?id=3390& wit_id=7214).

3. *Al Maqaleh* v. *Gates*, 605 F.3d 84 (D.C. Cir. 2010).

4. "Remarks by the President on National Security," Washington D.C., May 21, 2009 (www.whitehouse.gov/the_press_office/Remarks-by -the-President-On-National-Security-5-21-09/).

5. "Remarks by the President in State of the Union Address," Washington D.C., January 27, 2010 (www.whitehouse.gov/the-press-office/ remarks-president-state-union-address).

6. David Kris, "Law Enforcement as a Counterterrorism Tool," address at the Brookings Institution, June 10, 2010.

7. Benjamin Powell, correspondence with author, June 28, 2010.

8. Richard A. Posner, *Not a Suicide Pact: The Constitution in a Time of National Emergency* (Oxford: Oxford University Press, 2006), p. 59.

9. Authorization for Use of Military Force, Public Law 107–40, September 18, 2001.

Chapter Two

1. Daphne Eviatar, "Debate Intensifies over Preventive Detention: Prominent Lawyers Urge Obama Administration Not to Create New Indefinite Detention Scheme," *Washington Independent*, July 2, 2009 (http://washingtonindependent.com/49457/left-leaning-lawyers-urge-caution-on-detention-policy).
2. 50 U.S.C. § 21
3. *Lockington* v. *Smith*, 15 F. Cas. 758, 759 (C.C. Pa. 1817). See also Gerald L. Neuman and Charles F. Hobson, "John Marshall and the Enemy Alien: A Case Missing from the Canon," *Green Bag 9*, no. 1 (2005), p. 38.
4. 40 Stat. 1651–52 (1917).
5. 40 Stat. 1716–19 (1917).
6. 40 Stat. 1772–73 (1918).
7. 6. Fed. Reg. 6321–25 (1941).
8. Robert R. Wilson, "Treatment of Civilian Alien Enemies," *American Journal of International Law 37*, no. 1 (1943), p. 30.
9. 335 U.S. 160 (1948).
10. Geneva Convention Relative to the Protection of Civilian Persons in Time of War, August 12, 1949.
11. U.S. Const., art. I, § 9, cl. 2.
12. See An Act to Enforce the Provisions of the Fourteenth Amendment to the Constitution of the United States, and for other Purposes, 17 Stat. 13 (1871), Section 4.
13. See An Act Temporarily to Provide for the Administration of the Affairs of Civil Government in the Philippine Islands, and for Other Purposes, 32 Stat. 691, 692 (1902), Section 5. For information on the invocation of this law, see *Fisher* v. *Baker*, 203 U.S. 174 (1906).
14. See Hawaiian Organic Act, 31 Stat. 141, 153 (1900), Section 67.
15. *Duncan* v. *Kahanamoku*, 327 U.S. 304 (1945).
16. The Bail Reform Act was passed as P.L. 98-473 (1984). The quoted language is codified at 18 U.S.C. § 3142(b).
17. See 18 U.S.C § 3142 (c) and 18 U.S.C § 3142 (e).
18. Tracey Kyckelhahn and Thomas H. Cohen, "Felony Defendants in Large Urban Counties: 2004," *Bureau of Justice Statistics Bulletin* (April 2008).
19. Act of September 24, 1789, ch. 20, § 33.

20. Anjana Malhotra, "Witness to Abuse: Human Rights Abuses under the Material Witness Law since September 11," *Human Rights Watch* 17, no. 2 (2005), p. 14.

21. Ibid., pp. 16 and 33.

22. See 18 U.S.C. § 3144. See also 18 U.S.C § 3142 (e).

23. Statement of Janet Napolitano before the Senate Committee on the Judiciary, *Hearing on Oversight of the Department of Homeland Security*, 111 Cong., 1 sess., May 6, 2009.

24. 8 U.S.C. § 1225 (b)(2)(A).

25. 8 U.S.C. § 1226 (a).

26. See *Zadvydas* v. *Davis*, 533 U.S. 678 (2001); *Clark* v. *Martinez*, 543 U.S. 371 (2005).

27. See Alan Dershowitz, "The Origins of Preventive Confinement in Anglo-American Law—Part I: The English Experience," *University of Cincinnati Law Review* 43, no. 1 (1974), p. 1.

28. Albert Deutsch, *The Mentally Ill in America: A History of their Care and Treatment from Colonial Times* (Columbia University Press, 1949), p. 419.

29. Ibid.

30. See Revised Code of Washington § 71.09.

31. See *Kansas* v. *Hendricks*, 521 U.S. 346, 360 (1997).

32. Monica Davey and Abby Goodnough, "Doubts Rise as States Hold Sex Offenders after Prison," *New York Times*, March 4, 2007.

33. 18 U.S.C. §§ 4247-4248.

34. *United States* v. *Comstock*, 551 F. 3d 274 (May 17, 2010).

35. See Cal. Welfare and Institutions Code §§ 3100-3111.

36. *Robinson* v. *California*, 370 U.S. 660 (1962).

37. For the definition of chemical dependency, see Revised Code of Wash. § 70.96A.020(4)(a). For the authorization for involuntary commitment, see § 70.96A.140(1).

38. Col. Revised Statutes § 25-1-316.

39. Col. Revised Statutes § 25-1-310(1)(a).

40. See press release, N.Y.C. Department of Homeless Services, "DHS Institutes 24-Hour Cold Weather Emergency Procedure," January 26, 2007 (www.nyc.gov/html/dhs/html/press/pr012607.shtml).

41. See 50 P.S. § 7302 (Pa. 2009).

42. *Hamdi* v. *Rumsfeld*, 542 U.S. 507 (2004).

43. *Boumediene* v. *Bush*, 553 U.S. 723 (2008).

Chapter Three

1. Transcript of Hearing, *Anam* v. *Obama*, No. 04-1194 (D.D.C. Dec. 14, 2009).
2. *Al Adahi* v. *Obama*, 2009 WL 2584685 (D.D.C. 2009).
3. *Al Adahi* v. *Obama*, 2010 WL 2756551 (D.C. Cir. 2010).
4. See, respectively, *Al Mutairi* v. *United States*, 644 F. Supp.2d 78 (D.D.C. 2009); *El Gharani* v. *Bush*, 593 F. Supp.2d 144 (D.D.C. 2009); *Mohammed* v. *Obama*, 689 F.Supp.2d 38 (D.D.C. 2009).
5. *Hamlily* v. *Obama*, 616 F. Supp.2d 63 (D.D.C. 2009).
6. *Al-Bihani* v. *Obama*, 590 F.3d 866 (D.C. Cir. 2010).
7. *Basardh* v. *Obama*, 612 F. Supp.2d 30 (D.D.C. 2009).
8. *Awad* v. *Obama*, 646 F. Supp.2d 20 (D.D.C. 2009).
9. *Awad* v. *Obama*, 608 F.3d 1 (D.C. Cir. 2010).
10. Del Quinten Wilber, "Detainee-Informer Presents Quandary for Government," *Washington Post*, February 3, 2009.
11. See *Basardh* v. *Obama*, 612 F. Supp.2d 30 (D.D.C. 2009).
12. *Al Ginco* v. *Obama*, 626 F. Supp.2d 123 (D.D.C. 2009).
13. *Al-Adahi* v. *Obama*, 2009 WL 2584685 (D.D.C. 2009).
14. *Al Adahi* v. *Obama*, 2010 WL 2756551 (D.C. Cir. 2010).
15. *Salahi* v. *Obama*, 2010 WL 1443543 (D.C. 2010).
16. *Al-Bihani* v. *Obama*, 590 F.3d 866 (D.C. Cir. 2010).
17. *Awad* v. *Obama*, 646 F. Supp.2d 20 (D.D.C. 2009).
18. *Ahmed* v. *Obama*, 613 F. Supp.2d 51 (D.D.C. 2009).
19. Transcript of Hearing, *Anam* v. *Obama*, No. 04-1194 (D.D.C. Dec. 14, 2009).
20. *Hatim* v. *Obama*, 677 F.Supp. 2d. 1 (D.D.C. 2009).
21. See, for example, *Ahmed* v. *Obama*, 613 F. Supp.2d 51 (D.D.C. 2009).
22. *Mohammed* v. *Obama*, 689 F.Supp.2d 38 (D.D.C. 2009).
23. *Al-Adahi* v. *Obama*, 2010 WL 2756551 (D.C. Cir. 2010).
24. *Awad* v. *Obama*, 646 F. Supp.2d 20 (D.D.C. 2009).
25. *Awad* v. *Obama*, 608 F.3d 1 (D.C. Cir. 2010).
26. *Basardh* v. *Obama*, 612 F. Supp.2d 30 (D.D.C. 2009).
27. *Hatim* v. *Obama*, 677 F.Supp.2d 1 (D.D.C. 2009).
28. *Awad* v. *Obama*, 646 F. Supp.2d 20 (D.D.C. 2009).
29. *Al Mutairi* v. *United States*, 644 F. Supp.2d 78 (D.D.C. 2009).
30. *Al Adahi* v. *Obama*, 2009 WL 2584685 (D.D.C. 2009).

31. *Mohammed* v. *Obama,* 689 F.Supp.2d 38 (D.D.C. 2009).
32. See, for example, *Al-Bihani* v. *Obama,* 590 F.3d 866 (D.C. Cir. 2010). See also See also *Al Adahi* v. *Obama,* 2010 WL 2756551 (D.C. Cir. 2010).
33. *Salahi* v. *Obama,* 2010 WL 1443543 (D.D.C. 2010).

Chapter Four

1. *Mahmoad Abdah* v. *Obama,* 2010 WL 2326041 (D.D.C. May 26, 2010).
2. Barack Obama, "Inaugural Address," Washington, January 20, 2009.

Chapter Five

1. See David A. Martin, "Refining Immigration Law's Role in Counterterrorism," in *Legislating the War on Terror: An Agenda for Reform,* edited by Benjamin Wittes (Brookings, 2009), p. 206. The Alien Terrorist Removal Court is codified at 8 U.S.C. §§ 1531-1537.
2. See Section 412 of Public Law 107-56.
3. David Kris, "Law Enforcement as a Counterterrorism Tool," address at the Brookings Institution, June 10, 2010.
4. Transcript of Hearing, *Anam* v. *Obama,* No. 04-1194 (D.D.C. Dec. 14, 2009).
5. *Al-Bihani* v. *Obama,* 590 F.3d 866 (D.C. Cir. 2010).
6. See the Terrorist Detention Review Reform Act, S. 3707, 111 Cong., 2 sess., introduced August 4, 2010.
7. Ibid. See Section 2, § 2256(b).
8. Benjamin Wittes and Colleen A. Peppard, "Designing Detention: A Model Law for Terrorist Incapacitation," published on the Brookings Institution website, June 26, 2009 (www.brookings.edu/papers/2009/0626_detention_wittes.aspx).

Chapter Six

1. Jane Mayer, "The Hard Cases: Will Obama Institute a New Kind of Preventive Detention for Terrorist Suspects?" *New Yorker,* February 23, 2009.

Index

154   *Index*

160   *Index*

Guantánamo detainees, 64, 91,
118–19; on health detentions, 49;
on immigration detentions, 47;
on involuntary statements, 77;
on preventive detention of enemy
combatants, 57; on sex offender
detentions, 50, 51

Taint, 79–81, 86
Taliban: evidence of membership or
support of, 74, 82–83; as subject
to noncriminal detention, 68
Targeted killings: and detention
policy, 23–24; and habeas corpus
reviews, 61; increased use of,
139; intelligence costs of, 27; and
international law, 26; moral costs
of, 6, 25–26
Torture and involuntary statements,
78
Trojan War, 38
Tuberculosis control, 52

Unlawful enemy combatants: and
acute emergency detentions in
U.S., 95, 98; in large number of

detainees scenario, 106; preven-
tive detention for, 35, 37–38,
56–57
Urbina, Ricardo, 80, 85–86
U.S. Court of Appeals for the D.C.
Circuit. *See* D.C. Circuit.
Vitiation of relationship with enemy
groups, 73–74, 84–85

War of 1812, 40
Warrantless wiretapping, 139, 144
Washington Post on detainee as
cooperating witness, 73
Washington state, sex offender
detentions in, 50
Wilson, Woodrow, 40
Wiretapping, 139, 144
Wittes, Benjamin, 17–18, 34, 134
World War I, 40
World War II, 40–41
Wrongful detentions, 106–7, 118

Yemeni detainees, 16–17, 104

Zazi, Najibullah, 102
Zubaydah, Abu, 97